INFRINGED

Are you a gun owner?
Know the law and your rights.

by
ALEXANDRIA KINCAID
Firearms Law Attorney

Cover photograph by Amanda Allard showing the author at the Idaho State Capitol building, with thanks to MCM Firearms for the use of their custom Winchester SX-AR 308. Cover design by Ralph Richardson and Janet Colburn. All rights reserved. No part of this book may be reproduced by any means without prior written permission of the publisher.

Published by Hidden Hollow Publishing, PO Box 2252, Eagle ID 83616

Printed in the United States of America

First Edition, First Printing

ISBN 978-0-9969175-0-6 (Hardback)

ISBN 978-0-9969175-3-7 (Softback)

ISBN 978-0-9969175-1-3 (ebook)

Acknowledgments:

My life and my outlook would not have been the same without my grandparents, who shared with me their first-hand accounts of living through World War II in Germany. Among many other things, their stories taught me to be thankful that I live in America. Their generous words of wisdom also taught me, at a very early age, about the dangers of an out-of-control government. I am grateful to my mom, who gave me the life I have had in America, for always being there for me, and for selflessly having my best interest in mind. I am also thankful for my dad, who gave me my first .22 and taught me how to shoot. Thank you to the many friends and family who supported me through this project, freely giving me feedback and honest opinions, and in particular, my entire team at Alex Kincaid Law, including my office manager, Dasha Mackrill, my reference guru, Kaleena Bluemer, and my editors, Jason Mackrill and Wendy Breckon.

Dedication:

To my loving husband, Eric.

Table of Contents

Section III: Where You Can & Cannot Take a Firearm, and How to Take It There Lawfully

Section IV: The Second Amendment's Ultimate Protection—Defending Your Life with Deadly Force

About the Author

Alexandria Kincaid is a nationally renowned firearms law attorney. Her expertise of the gun laws is respected by gun owners, gun businesses, and gun rights organizations across America. In addition to gun owners, her clients include well-known firearms and firearms-accessories manufacturers. Alex is a contributing writer for the American Shooting Journal.

Alex's history with firearms began when she was a young child, when her law enforcement father taught her to shoot at the age of five. During her career, she has relied on her firearms for self-protection amidst threats from the criminals she prosecuted while serving as an elected District Attorney. Her favorite firearms are WWII collectibles, and her favorite shooting activity involves long-distance challenges from the deck at her home in Idaho.

WHY I WROTE THIS BOOK

Our right to keep and bear arms has been infringed. We live in a world where ISIS followers publicly behead Christians, and common murderers kill the innocent out of anger, for fun, or for a few dollars. Americans depend upon our personal firearms to defend against these real-life monsters. Yet, we are disarmed every day by our own government when we engage in common, necessary behaviors such as traveling across state lines or going to work. Gun owners who are caught violating these restrictive gun laws are criminalized by our justice system and jailed.

It has been my experience as both a prosecutor and a civil law attorney that too many responsible gun owners unintentionally violate gun laws they do not even know exist. Seemingly innocent behavior is turned criminal by our legal system. Continuing to carry with an expired permit or giving a gun to a family member can land an unsuspecting gun owner with a criminal conviction, jail time, probation, fines, and . . . no gun.

Our state and federal governments have created so many laws restricting the possession and transfer of firearms that law-abiding citizens, attorneys, and other professionals are left confused about the legality of everyday occurrences. Even worse, the laws are constantly and quickly changing. Judges disagree on the interpretation of the Second Amendment, resulting in cases being decided one way on one side of the country and another way on the other side.

Every move we make with our firearms is regulated, and compliance is a tricky business. While I am a staunch advocate for the Second Amendment, this book is not intended to be a persuasive work outlining the history and reasoning behind the Second Amendment. Those books have already been well-written.[1]

Gun owners need a book to help us understand the system of guns laws, so we will think about ordinary, but heavily regulated, every day behavior that puts us at risk of committing an accidental felony.

Whether you have one firearm for hunting or self-defense, or hundreds of firearms in a custom, walk-in gun vault, gun owners have at least one thing in common: A valid concern about exercising our Second Amendment right without losing this right, or our guns, in the future. This book empowers every gun owner with the necessary knowledge to stay safe, legal, and alive.

Regardless of where you live in America, this book will help you understand:

- How to sell or give a gun to someone else without breaking the law;

- How to transfer or ship firearms across state lines;

- When you can buy a gun for another person;

- Who cannot possess a gun and why "possessing" is different from "owning;"

- How to travel legally with your firearm;

- When you can take your gun to work;

- How seniors can keep their gun rights, even if they need help managing their finances;

- How a gun trust can protect you, your family, and your guns;

- How the American legal system works and why the gun laws are constantly evolving;

- When you need a federal firearms license (FFL) and how to get one;

- What you need to know about using deadly force to protect your life;

- And much more!

Personal Message from Alex Kincaid

My passion for firearms came early and from three important areas in my life.

I was one of those lucky kids who was born and raised in a home where guns were "around." My dad served in law enforcement for over 30 years, and in those days, there were no trigger locks or fancy gun safes. My siblings and I were taught responsibility because it was a matter of life or death. It was also important that we learned how to shoot guns. I learned to shoot when I was five, and have enjoyed the sport ever since.

The second area of my life was less fun and a bit more harrowing. When I began prosecuting criminals, I began receiving threats. It was during this time of my life that I took self-defense training seriously and obtained permission to carry a gun in the courthouse. I felt much safer with my Walther PPK hidden under my suit jackets and knowing I was an accurate shot.

From my prosecution days, I also led the major crimes team. I prosecuted homicides and other firearms-related offenses. I led the investigations to determine whether shootings were murder or the lawful use of deadly force. This experience aided me in teaching others about the laws pertaining to deadly force. What I did not anticipate was that years later, after I had left the District Attorney's office and was in private practice, I would be attacked in my own home.

This brings me to the third reason I am so passionate about firearms and self-defense training, and why I fervidly want to teach others how to avoid this type of a situation. I was physically attacked when I was completely unprepared to defend myself. While this was a very traumatic event in my life, it also instilled in me the passion to help others prevent this from happening to them.

I enjoy teaching men and women alike about self-defense. We all need to be prepared, and we need to do it with extensive training and knowledge. Everything I do, from being an instructor to being an attorney, is about making this happen. I hope this book will help you and motivate you, and I thank you for reading.

My best . . .

Alexandria

Section I:
The American Legal System

1

SPEAKING ABOUT THE GUN LAWS . . .

If your state's legislature passed a law banning all handguns and semi-automatic rifles, would you know how to explain why such a law violates the Second Amendment? Would you know how to fight back?

Do you know why so many restrictive gun laws have been passed and are deemed "constitutional"?

If you wish to research whether giving a firearm to someone in another state is legal, and if so, how to do it, do you know which laws (state, federal, statutes, case law) to review for the answers?

Can you explain how an executive order issued by the United States President or a state governor differs from other laws?

Do you know how judges, instead of Congress or our state legislatures, make laws?

Understanding the basic structure of our legal system is necessary to understanding the gun laws. This first section, while somewhat technical, lays the basic foundation for understanding the specific gun laws we review in later chapters.

2

Why I Wish Clients Would Not Rely on Google for Answers to Legal Questions

Gun owners often do just enough research on a legal question to be dangerous. They Google a topic on the internet and find the answer according to one set of rules (such as federal law) but fail to research the other, equally applicable, set of rules (such as their state's laws). There can be multiple laws that apply to any given situation. Laws are enacted by federal and state legislatures, as well as by city or county governments. In addition, these laws are interpreted on a case by case basis by federal and state appellate judges whose decisions add to the statutory laws.

Our federal, state, and local laws are not like a pyramid with local on the bottom and federal on the top. In other words, state laws are not a subset of federal laws. They are a completely different set of rules, and you are expected to know and comply with both state and federal laws. That is where many law-abiding gun owners unintentionally get into trouble. For example, it is legal to own certain machine guns under federal law. Your state law, however, may make you a criminal for possessing any kind of machine gun.

The federal system applies to you, regardless of which state you call home or where you may travel. Different states have different systems, and you must comply with each state's laws where you may travel with your firearm (with limited exceptions), regardless of where you normally live.

It is important for gun owners to understand how these different laws work together in our American legal system, so you will see the traps and avoid them.

3

WHERE DID THAT LAW COME FROM? UNDERSTANDING STATUTES, CASE LAW, AND THE COURT SYSTEM

Most laws are either statutes (created by a legislative body) or case law (created by a court).

A statute is a bill passed into law by Congress or a state legislature. Gun owners must comply with all federal statutes. An example of a federal statute is the Gun Control Act. This federal law, among other things, lists classes of people who cannot possess a firearm, such as convicted felons. In addition to federal statutes, gun owners must also comply with state statutes. An example of a state statute is a state's own criminal law that makes it a crime for a felon to possess a firearm.

Case law, on the other hand, is a court's ruling in a lawsuit that has been reduced to a written court "opinion." Case law can interpret the meaning of a statute (lawyers often argue about what words mean). For example, a judge might decide what constitutes "possession" of a firearm if it is not clearly explained in a statute—we discuss the meaning of this word later in this book. Another example of case law would be when a court decides whether or not a law is constitutional, such as restrictions on a person's ability to carry a firearm, whether a woman has a right to choose to have an abortion, or whether homosexuals have a right to marry. These are classic examples of "judge-made" laws, where the law is already written, but a court decides how to apply that law to a specific situation.

The American court system consists of tiers, or "levels," of courts that decide cases. You have to move through this system (appeal to the next highest level) to get to the highest court in either the state or federal system.

The first tier of courts consists of trial courts, where the facts and evidence are produced to a judge or jury, the "decider of fact." The trial court is where the parties make arguments, question witnesses, produce documents or other evidence, and the outcome of the case is decided for the first time. When you watch a typical television or movie courtroom scene, you are watching the portrayal of a trial court. If a gun owner has filed a lawsuit alleging that a state law violates the protections of the state constitution, the gun owner will produce evidence and witnesses to show why the gun owner's rights were violated. The gun owner may testify and examine (question) and cross-examine witnesses. A judge or jury will then make a decision based on the evidence presented. "Trial" is the court proceeding where both parties in a lawsuit (usually a plaintiff and defendant) testify or put forth other evidence about their case.

The second tier of courts consists of an initial appellate system, where the appellate court reviews a trial court's decision. If the gun owner lost the case at the trial level, the gun owner might file an "appeal" with the next level of court. An appellate court consists of a panel of judges or justices who decide legal questions. A legal question is a question of law when the facts are already decided. An example of a legal question would be whether a police officer's search of your car violated your rights. A factual question would be whether the police officer found a gun in your car. Attorneys make arguments in an appellate court based on the law and the facts that were presented at trial. Witnesses are not questioned in an appellate court. Instead, the lawyers and the court rely on the evidence and witnesses that were presented in the trial court. The court can decide to "uphold" the trial court's decision, "overturn" the trial court's decision, or "remand" the trial court's decision, which means sending the case back to the trial court to clarify certain items.

The third and top tier of courts is a higher level of appellate court, which reviews the lower appellate court's decision and makes a final decision. If a party disagrees with the initial appellate court's decision (and has the money to file an additional appeal), that person can get one more shot at the final decision for the case. Even judges can disagree on their interpretation of the laws—a judge in one court might decide the facts one way, and a judge in another court may decide the exact same case differently.

For example, there are nine United States Supreme Court Justices, and even though they all hear the exact same set of facts, they are often split on how they interpret those facts and apply them to the law. This phenomenon is why I caution gun owners that the laws are constantly changing, and the laws differ depending on location.

Understanding which level of court decided a case can be determined from the case's title or "caption." The caption of "*District of Columbia v. Heller*, 554 U.S. 570 (2008)" tells you that the parties to the case are the District of Columbia (defen-

7

dant and appellant) and Mr. Heller (plaintiff and respondent to the appeal). Mr. Heller filed the original lawsuit against the District of Columbia, and won. The District of Columbia filed the appeal. The caption also tells you that if you want to find the court's written opinion (the case law), you will find it in volume 554 of the United States Reports at page 570. The United States Reports contain the opinions of the United States Supreme Court.

4

THE POWER OF THE PRESIDENT'S PEN: UNDERSTANDING EXECUTIVE ORDERS

The stroke of the American President's pen can create new law without approval of the courts or Congress. Every president has used executive orders, but some have been more creative in using them than others. President Obama brought the power of his pen to light when he publicly announced that with respect to gun control, he intended to act where Congress would not. His proclamation excited gun haters and incited gun owners.

How can the American people tell when a president exceeds the authority of the executive office with an executive order? The bounds of the president's pen power remain unclear. While executive orders are usually directed at a governmental agency, they also affect the American people. If a president issues an order, the order is the law of the land until our legislative or judicial branch nullifies it.

Most presidents have issued executive orders to direct and manage federal governmental operations, not replace Congress and the will of the American people by enacting gun control. For example, a president may take emergency action as Commander in Chief of the United States Armed Forces, or take executive action after Congress has specifically provided authority for the president to do so. Other times, presidents have acted on their own accord, relying on an alleged grant to take "executive action" under the United States Constitution.

However, the United States Constitution does not provide clear authority for executive orders, and the orders issued by our presidents have rarely cited a specific constitutional authority. Instead, presidents have relied upon three different clauses in the Constitution to justify their actions:

1. The "Vestiture Clause," which states, "The executive Power shall be vested in a President of the United States of America;"[2]

2. The "Take Care Clause," which states that the president "shall take Care that the Laws be faithfully executed;"[3] and

3. The "Commander in Chief Clause," which states that the president "shall be Commander in Chief of the Army and Navy of the United States, and of the Militia of the several States, when called into the actual Service of the United States."[4]

In an attempt to curb tyranny, Representative Rand Paul introduced the Separation of Powers Restoration Act in 2001, and the Separation of Powers Restoration and Second Amendment Protection Act of 2013. Unfortunately, neither bill became law. If either of these bills had passed, they would have required that a president cite the specific provision of the Constitution or some other law giving him the power to issue the order. In addition, these laws would have specifically limited what types of orders the president could issue, and would have made it easier for citizens to fight unlawful executive orders in court.

As it stands now, presidents continue to use executive orders to influence issues in hundreds of areas. Notable executive orders have addressed war-related activities. For example, President Franklin D. Roosevelt ordered the confinement of Japanese-Americans to internment camps following the bombing of Pearl Harbor in December 1941.[5] More recently, after the 9/11 attacks, President George W. Bush declared a national emergency, called members of the U.S. Armed Forces' Ready Reserve to active duty,[6] and blocked the financing of terrorist organizations.[7] The Homeland Security Department was also originally created by an executive order issued by President Bush.[8]

It is noteworthy that executive orders can also be used by governors to direct state agencies, often in response to emergencies, but also to promote the governors' own regulatory and social policies. In 2015, the governor of Virginia issued an executive order "to prevent gun violence," which includes, among other things, a ban on firearms inside state government buildings.

One argument against executive orders is that by issuing them, a president overrides the checks and balances of our system of government. Actually, the checks and balances system still exists, but in a different order. For example, if Congress passes a law, the President can refuse to sign it (veto), or the courts can overrule it (by declaring it unconstitutional). Similarly, if a court decides a case, Congress can pass a law that overrides the judge-made law. In the same vein, if a president issues an executive order, Congress or the courts can nullify the order. You can see that even when a president issues an

11

executive order, our system of checks and balances still exists, it is just a difference of which branch of government created the law, and which branches have the ability to overturn the law. However, whether executive orders were anticipated by America's Founders is another discussion.

5

THE JURY OF YOUR PEERS—TWELVE STRANGERS WHO MAY HATE GUNS

If you are unlucky enough to be an accidental felon, you may think a jury of your peers at trial will understand that your violation of the law was unintentional and that these reasonable jurors will not hold you accountable for a technical law violation.

Take a deck of cards, spread it out, pick twelve cards, and you have your jury. You may get a good hand; you may not. While I am proud of my trial record, I frequently caution my clients when we are headed for trial that a jury pool is like a deck of cards, and going to trial can be like playing poker. Yes, lawyers get to question potential jurors at the beginning of a trial. Yes, lawyers can excuse jurors for no reason or "for cause." The reality is that most hard-working, conservative Americans have jobs, and sitting on a jury hurts their ability to provide for their families. These desirable jurors (depending on which side of a case you are arguing) sometimes try to avoid jury duty. Gun-hating Americans who want to be on a jury may lie during questioning so they can decide the case. Attorneys even employ experts to help them pick the "right" jurors for their side of a case. Jury selection is an art, a science, and a game. You are *never* safe with a jury.

What is the jury supposed to do? A jury's function is to serve as the trier of fact. In other words, each side presents evidence to try to prove their case, and the jury decides what is true and not true. Another way of thinking about this process is the jury "tries" pieces of evidence on to see which one fits the story. Evidence is not fact. Evidence is what lawyers use to prove facts. The jury exists to hear the evidence presented to it by the parties or their lawyers during a trial and to make a decision based on the jurors' collective interpretation of those facts and how the law should apply to them. The jury decides who is lying and who is not. The law is given to juries by judges who read "jury instructions" to the juries after all the evidence has been presented.

If you ever get the chance to sit on a jury, I encourage you to do so. While it can be a hardship to miss work or find daycare for children, it is an incredible privilege that we enjoy as Americans. Many jurors enjoy the experience and the knowledge they acquire of the legal system by participating in the process.

A couple of other important points to understand about our court system include the "rules of evidence" and the difference between a "legal" question and a "factual" question. People frequently describe to me scenarios, usually about when they might use their firearm to defend themselves, and ask me for a black and white answer on whether their behavior would be lawful. The questions usually go something like this:

Let's say I'm in a parking lot and I see some guys who appear to be gang members in a group. Can I show them my gun to make sure they know to stay away?

14

What if one of them starts walking towards me? What if one of them shoves me, can I point my gun at him? What if he kicks me in the shin? What if he shows me a gun?

The answer from me is most commonly, "It depends." The reason lawyers cannot always give a firm answer to a fact pattern is because the answer really does depend on the entire factual situation. There may be many other facts to this story that the jury would get to hear.

A factual question is a question decided by a jury based on the evidence that the jury is allowed to hear. Juries do not get to hear everything. Certain facts, such as the gang member's five prior convictions for assault, may never be learned by the jury due to the rules of evidence. What if the guy asking me the above question was a 300 pound motorcycle gang member who at the time of the incident was wearing a Hells Angels jacket? What if a 110 pound 25 year old woman asked me the same question? What if the jury deciding the case was all white or all women or all non-gun owners?

You also cannot underestimate the effect from the biases and opinions of the individual jurors—the people making the decision as to whether your version of the facts, or your opponent's version, is true. One jury could decide the same fact pattern differently from another jury. One poorly chosen juror can sway an entire jury, right or wrong.

During a trial, juries get a brief introduction to the law and are expected to apply the law correctly in life and death situations. When I teach self-defense laws, I do so by reviewing the applicable jury instructions with my students or clients. Usually at the end of a trial, juries hear these specific instructions from the judge to help them understand the law and apply it to the facts of a case. Many states have model jury instructions. The judge might tell the jury that a person charged with murder is not guilty of murder if the jury reaches certain conclusions based on the evidence that was presented during the trial. For example, a jury instruction might say that a person who shot someone and is on trial for murder should be found not guilty if the person reasonably believed his or her life was in danger and another reasonable person standing in the shooter's shoes would have believed the same.

What can be particularly helpful about studying jury instructions is that the instructions combine the statutes with the interpretive case law. If you just read a statute, you will not necessarily know how your court interprets that statute when applying it to particular facts. For example, let us assume that your state's law allows you to use your firearm to defend yourself in your own home if there is an intruder in your home in the middle of the night. A court in your state has previously interpreted the word "home" to include any place in which you are staying the night (like a tent, a camper, or a hotel room). The jury instruction will often include an explanation that a "home" can be a place where someone is staying overnight, even if the stay is temporary. These comprehensive instructions help jurors, and gun owners who wish to be better prepared, understand the law so they can properly apply it to a case and decide the factual questions.

In contrast to factual questions decided by a jury, legal questions are for judges to decide. The jury decides what happened and when. The judge will apply the law and make legal decisions, such as whether to allow the jury to hear certain evidence, which jury instructions to use, and often, which sentence is applicable.

While the American legal system is designed to effect justice, knowing the law so you can avoid the "dealer handing you a jury" is always the best option.

6

How the Layers of Laws Work Together & What Happens When They Conflict

Most Americans know that the United States Constitution is the supreme law of the land. Every law in America, state and federal, must not contradict the protections afforded Americans by the United States Constitution.

However, under the Constitution, the states are also sovereign—meaning each state is its own master. The federal government makes its own laws, and the state governments make their own laws. The federal government is its own entity and is designed to work on behalf of all of the states collectively, but it does not make state law and cannot tell state governments what to do, except in limited circumstances.

Even when Congress cannot tell states what to do by passing a controlling law, Congress still owns the power of persuasion: federal money. Ever wonder why the drinking age across America is 21? Or why some states have a process funded by Congress to restore gun rights for rehabilitated, but previously mentally ill people while others do not? It comes down to carrots held out by Congress to state governments: Do as Congress wishes (i.e. raise the state drinking age to 21), and get the funding (i.e. highway money); do not take the carrot, and lose out on

19

the federal handout.

Theoretically, however, the federal government will only intervene with a state's laws if the state law violates the Constitution of the United States. To see how this intervention works, let us assume the California state legislature passes a law that completely bans any kind of firearm ownership by California residents. Under this circumstance, a California resident could file a lawsuit in federal court. The complaining California resident could request that the federal court tell the State of California that the ban is unconstitutional, because it violates the provisions of the United States Constitution as contained in the Second Amendment. If the federal court decided that such a law did not violate the United States Constitution, then the person filing the lawsuit (the plaintiff) could appeal the case to a higher court—the Ninth Circuit Court of Appeals (the first layer of federal appeals courts that will review a lower federal court case coming out of California). If the Ninth Circuit Court of Appeals also said the law did not violate the Second Amendment to the United States Constitution, then the plaintiff could appeal to the United States Supreme Court.

The Supreme Court only reviews cases when the question at stake is a federal issue. An issue can be federal if it is tied to the Constitution of the United States. If the question is strictly about a state law and there is no federal Constitutional issue, then the court of last resort is the state's own highest court.

In our example, the plaintiff is arguing that the law violates the protection given by the Second Amendment of the United States Constitution, thus allowing the United States Supreme Court to decide the case.

You may have heard of the Supremacy Clause of the United States Constitution. The Supremacy Clause states:

This Constitution, and the Laws of the United States which shall be made in Pursuance thereof; and all Treaties made, or which shall be made, under the Authority of the United States, shall be the supreme Law of the Land; and the Judges in every State shall be bound thereby, any Thing in the Constitution or Laws of any State to the Contrary notwithstanding.[10]

The Supremacy Clause means that if state and federal laws conflict, the federal law controls, so long as the law does not violate the United States Constitution. But if state and federal laws do not conflict, they can co-exist, and you must obey both laws.

State firearms laws are often more restrictive than the federal laws. This does not mean the laws necessarily conflict—it means that the state is simply imposing more rules on your right to keep and bear arms than the federal government.

Let us look at the government's regulation of alcohol as a comparison to the regulation of firearms. Alcohol is regulated by the federal government, but also by each state's government. Federal law requires that you have permission, via a licensing procedure through the Bureau of Alcohol, Tobacco, Firearms, and Explosives to operate a home distillery. In other words, it is illegal to make your own moonshine at home unless you have followed the federal laws and obtained the appropriate license. State laws also regulate the sale of alcohol, which can restrict where and when you can purchase the finished product of moonshine. This scenario explains why you may be able to buy moonshine at Costco in California, but you have to go to a special, state licensed liquor store to purchase the same moonshine in Idaho.

Applying this analogy to firearms might look like this: Under federal law, you will need permission from the federal government (the Bureau of Alcohol, Tobacco, Firearms and Explosives, or the ATF) to build a silencer (suppressor) in your garage. Even if you have permission from the federal government, your state's laws may make the possession of suppressors illegal. If you live in California, federal law would allow you to manufacture a suppressor, but California law will not.

Another example of the interplay between state and federal law would be speed limits. The state governments set all of the speed limits in their own states. At the time of this writing, the maximum freeway speed in Montana is 75 miles per hour, but it is 80 miles per hour in Idaho, and 65 miles per hour in Oregon. Each speed limit is a separate state law that you have to know and obey as soon as you cross the border into the next state. State firearms laws are no different. If you take your firearm from one state to another, it is crucial that you know the applicable firearm laws for every state in which you travel if you want to avoid the "accidental felony."

An excellent example of how state and federal laws can conflict is the legalization of marijuana by some state governments. Marijuana, under federal law, is still a controlled substance. In some states, people can possess or even sell marijuana right in front of a police officer and not be prosecuted under state law. BUT, if a person possesses or sells marijuana in front of an FBI agent in those same states, the FBI agent can arrest the drug user or dealer, and the federal government can prosecute the person in federal court. Gun owners also need to know that even though a state's law may legalize marijuana, the ATF will still deem a medical or recreational marijuana user as someone who cannot possess a firearm under federal law (more on this later), and can prosecute you for smoking a doobie and possessing a firearm at the same time.

Note that some states allow smaller governmental bodies (such as cities or counties) to pass additional firearms laws. A common example would be a city ordinance that prohibits people from shooting inside city limits. These local laws are simply laws made by the different divisions within a state, such as counties, townships, cities, and towns, and they can vary as you travel through the state. Apart from the U.S. Constitution, each state also has its own constitution, and every local law written within that state has to be in accordance with the state constitution as well as the U.S. Constitution.

Federal, state, and local laws can have different requirements, and violation of any of these laws can carry criminal penalties (fines and jail or prison time).

7

WHAT HAPPENS IF YOU BREAK BOTH STATE & FEDERAL LAWS?

You may have heard that you cannot be charged twice for the same crime. You actually can be charged twice for the same behavior: once for breaking state law and once for breaking federal law.

Consider an example where you inherit a fully-automatic firearm that your grandfather brought to the United States after serving in World War II. After his funeral, your grandmother gives you this valuable heirloom, and tells you how your grandfather wanted to make sure you received it. The problem is, the firearm was never registered with the ATF. Another problem is that your state does not allow civilians to own machine guns. If you take this heirloom home, you have violated the federal law known as the National Firearms Act and your state's law.

If your behavior violates both state and federal law, the state authorities can prosecute you for the state law violation (unlawful possession of a machine gun because machine guns are not allowed in your state), and the federal authorities can prosecute you for the federal law violation (you possessed an unregistered machine gun, which is contraband). This dual prosecution (known as the dual sovereignty doctrine) is possible, because as you read earlier, state and federal are two different jurisdictions. One is not a subset of the other.

I witnessed people being prosecuted twice for the same behavior a number of times during my time serving as a district attorney. These double prosecutions would commonly happen in drug and firearms related cases. A drug dealer would violate state drug and firearms laws, and the district attorney's office would prosecute him for violating the state's criminal laws. The drug dealer would be convicted and sentenced to a term in state prison for committing the state crimes. Months or even years later, this same criminal would be re-arrested by federal authorities and prosecuted for the same drug-dealing and unlawful firearm activity, which also violated the federal drug and firearms laws. If convicted under the federal system, this drug dealer would face additional fines and prison time in a federal penitentiary. These separate cases, state and federal, were filed based on the drug dealer's singular action. In other words, he was arrested for the charges and prosecuted by the state authorities and then separately prosecuted by the federal authorities.

8

THE PREEMPTION DOCTRINE: WHY THAT SIGN AT THE CITY PARK PROHIBITING FIREARMS MAY BE ILLEGAL

Some state laws specifically prohibit smaller governmental bodies, such as cities or counties, from passing any firearms related laws. However, these laws do not always keep these smaller governments in line. In fact, so many illegal local laws have been passed that national gun rights organizations such as the Second Amendment Foundation (SAF) and specific state grassroots organizations have devoted much effort to forcing cities and counties to comply with the state laws. These organizations have been in the news over the last few years for their "preemption projects."

Recall our discussion of the Supremacy Clause of the United States Constitution in chapter 6. The federal preemption doctrine means that a federal law enacted by Congress in pursuance of its constitutionally authorized powers will trump or "preempt" a conflicting state law. The reason is that certain matters are deemed to be of such a national, as opposed to local, character that federal laws preempt or take precedence over state laws related to those matters.

This "trumping" of regional laws works at the state level as well. Preemption occurs when a state law conflicts with a local ordinance on the same subject. In such a case, the state law will preempt, or trump, the local ordinance. Preemption laws differ amongst the states—some states allow local laws, others do not. It is important to know what your specific state's preemption statute allows, because if your state's laws allow local firearms laws to be passed, you must comply with the laws created by the cities and counties where you live and travel, unless and until they are proven unconstitutional.

If a state legislature enacts gun control legislation, and the intent of the legislation is to occupy the field of gun control, then a city is preempted (prohibited) from enacting its own gun control ordinance. A common violation of state preemption law occurs when a city enacts an ordinance prohibiting firearms in certain locations such as city offices or parks, when the state law does not give the lower governmental entity that authority.

A state preemption statute may also define what recourse is available for violations of the state's laws. At least one state (Florida) has a law that punishes local government officials who knowingly and willfully violate the state's firearms preemption statute.[11] Without a good preemption law in place, government officials who are against firearms simply create illegal laws prohibiting guns and ignore the public outcry to eliminate these illegal laws. It can be difficult for a person to obtain justice or get the illegal laws changed. Anti-gun government officials are even getting creative in trying to get around the preemption laws, by posting signs "requesting" that you not bring a gun inside a government building, rather than stating that guns are banned. Such signs are, of course, misleading to the unsuspecting gun owner who does not want to violate the law and is inclined to

28

obey a sign, whether it is a "demand" or a "request."

Second Amendment organizations have recognized this illegal behavior and have worked to educate government officials about the preemption doctrine. These organizations are making city officials aware of violations of state laws, and asking them to bring their local ordinances into compliance with state law and to remove illegal "no firearms" signs. They are demanding that signs touting unlawful ordinances be removed, such as signs on buildings or at parks that claim firearms are not allowed, when, according to state law, they are allowed.

The Second Amendment Foundation has led the preemption project at a national level. While the SAF has not expanded its project to all states, state organizations are taking action where the SAF has not. The effort by state gun rights organizations has been very successful, with most communities responding favorably by changing their ordinances and removing signs prohibiting firearms.[12]

9

WHY THE U.S. CONSTITUTION ONLY PROTECTS YOU SOME OF THE TIME

The Constitution protects us from the government—NOT private citizens. The Second Amendment protects our right to keep and bear arms against a tyrannical government.

A business owner, however, can usually tell you that you are not allowed to bring a firearm onto the business's private property.

To understand why the business owner has this power, think about your own home. You have the right to tell other people what they can and cannot do on your own property. The same rule applies to private property owned by a business. If your employer has a policy that you cannot bring firearms to work, the Second Amendment does not prevent your employer from firing you if you bring a gun to work. Consider the Duck Dynasty saga where star Phil Robertson was fired for his comments about the gay lifestyle. The television network did not violate the First Amendment by firing him, because a television network is not the government. Phil Robertson was NOT protected by the First Amendment in this situation.

If you live in a state where it is legal to openly carry a firearm into a government building (such as a city hall or the capitol building) but you are asked to leave while doing so, your right has been violated. But if you carry a gun into a privately owned grocery store where the owner has posted that firearms are not allowed, your Second Amendment right to keep and bear arms has not been violated because the government does not own that store. Another person owns the store, and that person gets to set the rules and can tell you not to bring a gun inside the store.

10

SIMPLE WORDS WITH COMPLICATED MEANINGS: DO YOU KNOW WHAT A FIREARM IS?

One of the mechanisms used by judges who want to change the meaning of existing law is to change the meaning of the words used in the law. Most people probably think they know what a "firearm" is, or what a "person" is, or what "possession" means. Most gun owners also think they know what the word "infringed" means. However, after lawyers, judges, and legislators are finished with the law, words you think you can define can mean something entirely different than the plain meaning of those words.

In this chapter, I illustrate this concept with a few key words in gun law lexicon.

Firearm

Most gun owners think they know what a "gun" is. But the word "gun" is rarely used in the law. The word "firearm" is used instead, and the meaning of the word can differ greatly depending on which law you are applying.

Some laws define parts of a firearm

> Many people are surprised to learn that what constitutes a "firearm" depends on which law you are applying.

as a firearm, or certain types of explosives or firearm suppressors as firearms. A firearm might be a firearm under federal law, but may not be a firearm under state law (or vice versa). MAKE SURE YOU KNOW WHETHER YOUR "FIREARM" *IS* A FIREARM.

For example, under federal law, the "receiver" in the picture is a firearm, the suppressor (silencer) is a firearm, and, as we will see in a later chapter, small parts less than a couple of inches in length are considered machine guns. In contrast, firearms such as the muzzleloading rifle in the picture, are not necessarily considered firearms under the law.

A muzzleloader (or black powder rifle) is not a firearm under the definition in the *federal* law known as the National Firearms Act. However, it is a firearm under the definition in a different *federal* law known as the Gun Control Act—but it is excepted from the requirements of that law. A muzzleloader is also a firearm under the definitions found in many *state* laws.

I have spoken with more than one felon who thought he could own a muzzleloader because a muzzleloader is exempt from the requirements of the *federal* Gun Control Act, which is the federal law that prohibits a convicted felon from possessing a firearm. Information is easily spread around on the internet, and the word has been spread that a convicted felon can be in possession of a muzzleloader.

The unwary felon may not realize (and sometimes his public defender did not warn him) that his state's law may not similarly exclude muzzleloaders, making his possession of a muzzleloader illegal and prosecutable.

I have also been asked by gun owners whether they can

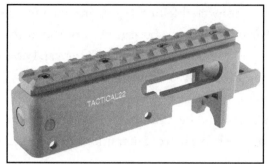

A 10/22 receiver. A firearm under federal law. Photo by Oleg Volk.

A silencer. A firearm under federal law. Photo by Oleg Volk.

A reproduction flintlock rifle. Not a firearm under federal law. Photo by Oleg Volk.

loan muzzleloaders to convicted felons. If you are not a felon, but you loan a firearm to a felon, you can be prosecuted for "aiding and abetting" the felon. Aiding and abetting can carry the same sentence (punishment) as the felon will get for unlawfully possessing the gun.

To help clarify how the definition of what constitutes a firearm differs, below are two different definitions of the word "firearm" under *federal* law:

Gun Control Act (GCA)

The GCA defines a "firearm" as:

(A) Any weapon (including a starter gun) which will or is designed to or may readily be converted to expel a projectile by the action of an explosive;

(B) The frame or receiver of any such weapon;

(C) Any firearm muffler or firearm silencer; or

(D) Any destructive device.[13]

Despite this broad definition, this federal law excludes "antiques" (a firearm that was actually made in or before 1898 and replicas of pre-1898 firearms) and any muzzle loading rifle, shotgun, or pistol, which is designed to use black powder and cannot use, or be readily converted to use, fixed ammunition. This exception to the definition is why you can order muzzle loaders on the internet and receive them in the mail without using a licensed dealer.

National Firearms Act (NFA)

The NFA is another *federal* law. Under the NFA, the term "firearm" has a very narrow definition, which includes only certain types of firearms:

- A shotgun with a barrel or barrels of less than 18 inches in length;
- A weapon made from a shotgun if, as modified, has an overall length of less than 26 inches or a barrel or barrels of less than 18 inches in length;
- A rifle with a barrel or barrels of less than 16 inches in length;
- A weapon made from a rifle if, as modified, has an overall length of less than 26 inches or a barrel or barrels of less than 16 inches in length;
- "Any other weapon" as defined in subsection (e) of 26 USC section 5845;
- A machinegun;
- A silencer; and
- A destructive device.

As you can see from the above definitions, federal laws can have different definitions from other federal laws, which can add to the confusion and frustration.

The following is an example of a state law defining the word "firearm": "Firearm means any deadly weapon capable of ejecting or propelling one (1) or more projectiles by the action of any explosive or combustible propellant, and includes unloaded firearms and firearms which are inoperable but which can readily be rendered operable."[14]

The following diagram shows how these two federal laws differ in defining the word "firearm," and how a state's laws may be even broader:

STATE FIREARMS
Any deadly weapon capable of ejecting a projectile by the action of any explosive, even if inoperable if it can readily be rendered operable.

GCA FIREARMS
• Pistols, Revolvers
• Rifles, Shotguns
• Frames or Receivers
• Machineguns
• Silencers, including parts
• Destructive devices
• All other weapons that expel a projectile by the action of an explosive

NFA FIREARMS
• Short-barrel Rifles
• Short-barrel Shotguns
• Machineguns
• Silencers, including parts
• Destructive devices
• Any other weapon

Person

A person is a living breathing human being, right? Wrong. A person is not just a human being. The Gun Control Act includes individuals, corporations, companies, associations, firms, partnerships, societies, or joint stock companies in the definition of "person." Trusts are not "persons" under the GCA.

The National Firearms Act includes individuals, certain trusts, estates, partnerships, associations, companies or corporations in its definition of "person."

Additionally, a state may have its own definition of the word "person" that may differ from the federal definitions.

Possession

Ownership and possession are not the same. If you are holding a firearm, you are *possessing* it, even though you may not *own* it. More specifically, if you are holding it, you are in "actual possession" of the firearm. Most criminal laws restrict "possession," not "ownership." It is technically possible in some instances for people who cannot possess firearms to legally "own" them.

The most problematic aspect of "possession" is that the courts have decided that a person can be convicted of illegally possessing a firearm even if they do not own it or are not holding it. The key to determining whether you are in possession is whether you have the right (or ability) to control the firearm. If you have the right to control the firearm, you can be deemed to be in "constructive possession" and prosecuted if you are not lawfully allowed to possess that firearm.

Another way to look at constructive possession is to think about a situation where you live with another person. If you live with someone who is not supposed to possess firearms, it is not alright for that person to live with you just because the firearms belong to you. If you live with a felon and you *own* the firearms but leave them where the felon can access them, you could be prosecuted for aiding and abetting a felon to *possess* firearms. The felon with whom you live could also be charged with the crime of felon *in possession* of a firearm. In other words, you could both be charged with a felony.

A gentleman once told me a story about his son, who was temporarily committed to a mental institution by a court process, because he was suicidal over the death of a loved one. When released, the son went to live with his father. The father owned many guns, and was worried about whether he could legally allow his son to live with him. The answer depends on how the father keeps the firearms. If he leaves guns lying around the house where the son can have control of (possess) them, then the dad is breaking the law. If the dad instead keeps the firearms locked in a safe to which the son does not know the combination, the son is not in possession. In the safe scenario, the father is taking the risk that a law enforcement officer, prosecutor, and jury will believe that the son did not know the combination to the safe . . . potentially risky business.

I am going to draw on my experience as the lead prosecutor for a couple of drug teams to further illustrate this point. When I and my law enforcement team would serve a search warrant on a suspected drug house, the homeowner did not need to be in the home, holding all the drugs to be charged with possession of controlled substances (illegal drugs). If we found drugs and paraphernalia in the drug dealer's car, and perhaps nothing inside the house, we could still arrest and prosecute him for possession. The reason is that under the law, *actual possession* is not required in order for that person to be charged with a crime. If the person violating the law is simply in *constructive possession* by exercising control over the illegal item (which he did because the drugs were in his car), that person is in "possession" and can be convicted of the crime.

Transfer

The term "transfer" means much more than selling a firearm. You might be transferring a firearm if you sell, assign, pledge, lease, loan, give away, or *otherwise dispose of* a firearm. Basically, if one person hands a firearm to another person, there may very well be, and likely is, a "transfer" that has taken

40

place, even if the transfer is temporary.

When you transfer a firearm, you must comply with state and federal laws. For instance, some transfers require that you use a licensed firearms dealer as an intermediary to complete (and record) the transfer. Transferring a firearm from one person to another, whether temporary or permanent, requires you to comply with many laws.

Conviction

The jurisdiction, state or federal, where a person was convicted of a crime will control what the definition of "conviction" means for that state and for the federal system of laws. If a person was convicted of a state crime in New York, New York law will define what the word "conviction" means for both federal and New York jurisdictions. In other words, the state law where the person is charged with the crime will determine whether one is "convicted" of a crime sufficient to revoke that person's right to possess a firearm under the *federal* system. Where a person has been convicted, no matter how long ago, dictates whether the person has any ability to erase the conviction from his or her record and regain his or her ability to own a firearm under both state and federal law.

However, other states may not recognize the originating state's definition of "conviction." For example, if the person in our New York example obtained a pardon of all his felony convictions, and moved to the state of Washington, Washington law may not recognize the pardons and instead, may deem the person to still be a convicted felon. This is an ongoing battle in certain states, and the states refusing to recognize other state's

41

pardons may be violating the U.S. Constitution. The legality of these state laws has not yet been decided by the courts.

The result is that if you are convicted of the crime of possessing a controlled substance in New York, but later have that conviction expunged from your record, federal law does not consider you "convicted." In addition, if you move to another state, you will need to make sure that whichever legal process "erased" any earlier convictions is recognized by your new home state.

11

Why Gun Laws Are Living, Breathing, Evolving Beasts

Under our current system, certain behavior may be legal in one location in this country, but criminal in another location. This situation is due to different states passing different laws and the appellate judges' different interpretations of those laws. A judge hearing a case in one court may decide that a law violates the Constitution, while a judge in another court may decide that the same law does not violate the Constitution. New federal and state cases determining the meaning of the Second Amendment continue to be decided, and unfortunately, continue to restrict gun owners' rights. The structure of our legal system explains this phenomenon.

Our Founding Fathers designed America to be a nation consisting of strong, individual state governments that would be united (as in the *United* States) by a weaker federal, or central, government. The idea was that the sovereign states would serve as "laboratories of democracy,"[15] and the federal government would exist as a subservient government responsible for functions like providing for the national defense and regulating interstate commerce. The federal government was designed by the Founders with the intent for it to play a supporting role in

the grand scheme of America, never to be the supreme governing body.

The Second Amendment to the United States Constitution
reads:

"A well regulated Militia, being necessary to the security
of a free State, the right of the people to keep and bear Arms,
shall not be infringed."[16] The title of this book is *"Infringed,"*
because so many laws have now been passed both by Congress
and by state legislatures that, despite the plain wording of the
Second Amendment, most gun owners would agree that our
Second Amendment protection has indeed been "infringed."

Gun owners often ask, "I don't get it—doesn't the
Constitution say 'shall not be infringed'? How can there be so
many laws that restrict the right to keep and bear arms?"

The short answer is that the interpreter of our
Constitution, the United States Supreme Court, has decided
that some restrictions on our right to keep and bear arms are
allowed. Justice Antonin Scalia wrote in the landmark case of
District of Columbia v. Heller (see Chapter 13 for more about this
important court case):

Like most rights, the Second Amendment right *is not
unlimited*. It is not a right to keep and carry any weapon
whatsoever in any manner whatsoever and for whatever purpose: For example, concealed weapons prohibitions have been upheld under the Amendment
or state analogues. The Court's opinion *should not be
taken to cast doubt* on longstanding prohibitions on the
possession of firearms by felons and the mentally ill,
or laws forbidding the carrying of firearms in sensi-

tive places such as schools and government buildings, or laws imposing conditions and qualifications on the commercial sale of arms.[17]

While the *Heller* decision was a victory for gun owners, Justice Scalia (whom I greatly admire) and the Supreme Court as a whole, unfortunately, left a great deal open to interpretation by the lower appellate courts.

The first problem with the quoted language is that it leaves open the question of what would constitute a constitutional restriction on the right to keep and bear arms. Only a few examples are given of lawful restrictions. These examples are the concealed carry laws, possession by felons, possession by the mentally ill, and possession in certain locations. Judges across the country have since found many other reasons to justify restricting our right to keep and bear arms.

The second problem with the vague language is that Justice Scalia's written court decision does not provide lower courts with guidance on what standard to use to determine whether a law is an unconstitutional infringement on the right to keep and bear arms.

Many court cases will interpret a law when there is no clear answer, setting a precedent for the lower courts (trial and lower appellate courts) to follow. In doing so, they will often give detailed examples or even create a definition so a lower court knows how to decide a case when the same subject comes up in its jurisdiction. Two possible consequences of leaving a law open to interpretation are inconsistency and injustice. We are now living these consequences across America.

For example, a case arose in Texas in which a federal

judge ruled that part of the federal Gun Control Act is unconstitutional.[18] The judge ruled that the part of the Gun Control Act
that prohibits a resident of one state from buying a handgun in
another state violates the potential buyer's Second Amendment
right to keep and bear arms. A similar lawsuit could be filed by
a potential handgun purchaser who wishes to purchase a handgun in Wisconsin. The Wisconsin plaintiff, however, may not
receive the same decision from the judge. The Wisconsin judge
may decide the case differently, even though the facts are similar (the plaintiff wishes to buy a handgun in a state other than
his home state) and the legal question is the same (Does the
Gun Control Act violate the would-be purchaser's right to keep
and bear arms?). The Wisconsin district court judge may decide
that the law banning the purchase of handguns in other states
is constitutional, because there is no bright line standard for
judges to use to decide upcoming Second Amendment cases.

Worse for gun owners, we have to be aware of which
courts decide that a law is unconstitutional. The case in Texas
only applies in Texas. After that case was decided, I was flooded
with inquiries from gun business owners asking if they could
now sell handguns to people who live in another state. The
answer is "NO," unless you live in the District of Texas. Even
then, the case may be appealed to a higher court and decided
differently a couple of years from now. When we hear about
"wins" in court through the media, it does not necessarily mean
that the law has changed in every jurisdiction. A case involving federal laws or the United States Constitution has to be
decided by the United States Supreme Court before gun owners throughout the United States can rely on the decision.

Despite this lack of clarity, gun owners have some certainty about what will constitute a violation of the laws we already have in place. In the next section, we review what we do know with more certainty (for now) about the federal gun laws passed by Congress.

SECTION II:

THE FEDERAL SYSTEM'S MOST VIOLATED GUN LAWS

12

EXACTLY WHEN DID THE INFRINGEMENT BEGIN?

The federal government began whittling away our Second Amendment protection with its first significant law in 1934, when Congress passed the National Firearms Act. Since then, we have seen the appearance of new, federal gun laws in regular succession. Like their predecessors, these laws are consistently precipitated by highly publicized, gun-related crimes.

The information in this chapter is designed to give you a brief outline of the history of the federal gun laws. Federal law applies to everyone across the states, so every responsible gun owner should have a basic understanding of the federal gun laws. Knowledge will not only allow you to better understand the rules, but will also help you speak intelligently and correctly in any discussions you may have with firearms prohibitionists.

The next few chapters provide an overview of the two federal laws that most commonly affect both individual gun owners and gun-related businesses. I will discuss the most significant features of each of these federal laws, and show you how you can avoid violating these laws and committing an "accidental felony."

FEDERAL GUN LAW TIMELINE:

- ▣ **1791 <u>Second Amendment Ratified</u>:** "A well regulated Militia, being necessary to the security of a free State, the right of the people to keep and bear Arms, shall not be infringed."

- ▣ **1871 <u>National Rifle Association Founded</u>:** Union soldiers Colonel William C. Church and General George Wingate found the NRA to "promote and encourage rifle shooting on a scientific basis." Civil War General Ambrose Burnside, who was also the former governor of Rhode Island and a U.S. Senator, serves as the organization's first president.

- ▣ **1934 <u>National Firearms Act (NFA)</u>:** Brought about after the St. Valentine's Day Massacre in 1929, and the attempted assassination of President Franklin D. Roosevelt, this law was intended to control the gangster culture created during Prohibition. The government hoped to eliminate machine guns from America's streets . . . by taxing them into oblivion. Other firearms were also targeted, and all of these weapons were available by mail order during this era. The transfer and manufacture of these targeted firearms slapped those involved with a $200 tax (approximately equivalent to $3,551.42 in 2015), and all transferees and manufacturers were required to fill out paperwork subject to Treasury Department approval. Signed into law by President Franklin D. Roosevelt.

- **1938 Federal Firearms Act**: "An Act to regulate commerce in firearms," this law created the original "FFL." Anyone manufacturing, selling, or importing firearms was required to obtain a Federal Firearms License from the Secretary of Commerce ($1 annual fee). These FFLs were also required to record the names and addresses of everyone who purchased guns from them and were prohibited from selling to those people who were convicted of certain crimes or lacked a permit. This law was superseded by the Gun Control Act of 1968.

- **United States v. Miller, 307 U.S. 174 (1939)**: After a citizen was caught with a sawed-off shotgun without having paid the NFA tax, he challenged whether the NFA's restrictions on gun ownership were constitutional under the Second Amendment. The United States Supreme Court decided that only weapons having a reasonable relationship to the effectiveness of a well-regulated militia under the Second Amendment are free from government regulation. Specifically, because the United States military was not using sawed-off shotguns, citizens are not allowed to possess them, unless they pay the NFA tax.

- **1968 Omnibus Crime Control and Safe Streets Act**: The Omnibus Crime Control Act prohibited interstate trade in handguns and increased the minimum age for buying handguns to 21. Title III of the Act set rules for obtaining wiretap orders. This legislation was soon followed by the Gun Control Act of 1968, which set forth additional gun control restrictions. Together with the

GCA, these laws replaced the 1938 Federal Firearms Act. Signed into law by President Lyndon B. Johnson.

◉ **1968 <u>Gun Control Act</u>:** The 1963 assassination of John F. Kennedy, who was killed by a mail-order gun that belonged to Lee Harvey Oswald, inspired this major revision of federal gun laws. The subsequent assassinations of civil rights leader Reverend Martin Luther King, Jr. and presidential candidate Robert Kennedy increased public outrage against the ownership of guns, and ensured the enactment of the Gun Control Act (GCA). The GCA requires sellers of firearms to obtain a federal firearms license (FFL), requires these licensees to keep more records, and prevents anyone from buying a handgun except in their home state. It also defines categories of people banned from possessing firearms (including felons, the mentally ill, and drug users). This law also outlaws mail order sales of firearms. Signed into law by President Lyndon B. Johnson

◉ **1972 <u>Bureau of Alcohol Tobacco and Firearms created</u>:** Enforcement of the Gun Control Act was given to the Department of the Treasury's Alcohol and Tobacco Tax Division of the IRS. Although the organization had existed for decades by this time, the federal government replaced the word "tax" in its title with the word "firearms," nearly doubled the agency's size, and created the Bureau of Alcohol, Tobacco and Firearms (the ATF).

◉ **1986 <u>Law Enforcement Officers Protection Act</u>:** This law was enacted to address the concern that civilians

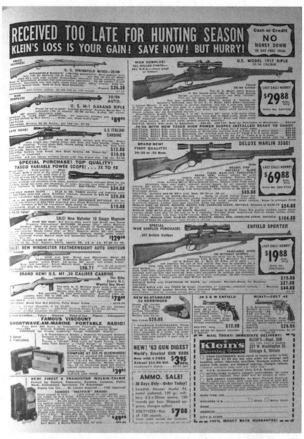

Full-page advertisement by Klein's Sporting Goods, of Chicago, in the February 1963 issue of American Rifleman magazine. The Warren Commission concluded that Lee Harvey Oswald purchased an Italian Carcano rifle and telescopic sight (left column, third from top) from this advertisement in March 1963, and used it to assassinate U.S. President John F. Kennedy in Dallas, Texas on November 22, 1963. The ad photo actually shows a telescopically modified Carcano TS, but by the time Oswald used the ad to order the "6.5 Italian Carbine," Klein's was shipping Carcano Model 91/38's. Thus, Oswald received the latter model.

would use armor piercing bullets to pierce the bullet-proof vests worn by law enforcement officers. The "LEOPA" made it illegal to manufacture, import, or sell armor piercing ammunition, or "cop-killer" bullets, which are capable of penetrating bulletproof clothing, except for government use, testing, or export. Signed into law by President Ronald Reagan.

◉ **1986 Firearms Owners' Protection Act**: The "FOPA" was passed in an effort to protect gun owners from an over-zealous ATF. It eased the Gun Control Act's restrictions on gun sales by allowing the sale of rifles and shotguns across state lines, allowing the mail-order of ammunition, and doing away with onerous record-keeping requirements for ammunition dealers. This law eased the rules for licensing, and allowed individuals to sell at gun shows under certain circumstances without a license. It also changed the definition of "machine gun" and banned civilians from possessing machine guns manufactured after 1986. Signed into law by President Ronald Reagan.

◉ **1988 Undetectable Firearms Act**: This law was proposed to address firearms such as the Glock 17, but after compromise to its original language, the law as passed did not affect any firearms in circulation at the time. The law makes it illegal to manufacture, import, sell, ship, deliver, possess, transfer, or receive any firearm that is not detectable as a firearm by walk-through metal detection or any firearm with major components that do not generate an accurate image before standard airport imaging technology. Signed into law by President Ronald Reagan.

- **1990 Gun Free School Zones Act:** Following highly publicized school shootings, this law was part of the Crime Control Act of 1990, and criminalized the possession of firearms in a school zone. It was later held unconstitutional by the United States Supreme Court, but Congress quickly rewrote the law to only apply it to firearms that have moved in or otherwise affect interstate commerce (which, of course, is true of almost every firearm in existence). Signed into law by President George H.W. Bush.

- **1994 Brady Handgun Violence Prevention Act:** This law was passed after the attempted assassination of President Ronald Reagan, which left his press secretary, Jim Brady, paralyzed for life. It is the law responsible for the required background checks when an individual buys a gun from a licensed gun importer, manufacturer, or dealer (unless an exception applies, such as the purchaser having a qualifying concealed carry permit). This law imposed a five-day waiting period for gun purchases, until the National Instant Criminal Background Check System (NICS) was implemented in 1998. Signed into law by President Bill Clinton.

- **1994 Violent Crime Control and Law Enforcement Act:** Proposed after the 101 California Street Shooting and the 1993 Waco Siege, this law is commonly referred to as the "Assault Weapons Ban." It is the largest crime bill in the history of the United States, consisting of 356 pages, and it banned the manufacture, possession, and importation of new semiautomatic "assault weapons" and large-capacity (anything over 10 rounds) ammunition feeding devices (magazines) for civilian use. This law ended in 2004, but we have since watched as states have passed similar laws, and Congress considered a permanent, more restrictive version in 2013, after the Sandy Hook school shooting. Signed into law by President Bill Clinton.

◾ **1996 Domestic Violence Offender Gun Ban**: Also known as the "Lautenberg Amendment," this law criminalizes the shipment, possession, and transfer of guns or ammunition by individuals convicted of misdemeanor domestic violence crimes, or who are under a restraining (protection) order for domestic abuse that falls within the criteria set by the Gun Control Act.[19] The act also makes it unlawful to knowingly sell or give a firearm or ammunition to such persons. Signed into law by President Bill Clinton.

◾ **1998 Brady Handgun Act**: The creation and implementation of the National Instant Criminal Background Check in 1998 spurred this law. It updated the 1994 version to require all gun dealers to run background checks on all potential buyers of firearms using the NICS system and eliminated the five day waiting period. Signed into law by President Bill Clinton.

◾ **2005 Protection of Lawful Commerce in Arms Act**: Before this law was passed, victims of firearms-related violent crimes successfully sued firearms manufacturers for negligence. These plaintiffs' theory was that the manufacturers and dealers should have known that the firearms would have been diverted to criminal use resulting in harm to other people. This law prevents manufacturers and dealers from being held liable for negligence on that theory. After the Sandy Hook and Aurora Theater shootings, victims attempted to sue the firearms manufacturers and failed, but efforts are still underway by gun control advocates to repeal this law. In a nod to gun control advocates, this law also mandates safety locks on all new handguns. Signed into law by President George W. Bush.

After nearly nine decades of this court and Congressional infringement upon our rights (with very few laws passed to protect the Second Amendment), the United States Supreme Court heard two landmark cases that hindered further infringement to some degree: *District of Columbia v. Heller*, 554 U.S. 570 (2008) and *McDonald v. Chicago*, 561 U.S. 742 (2010).

13

WHY EVERY GUN OWNER NEEDS TO UNDERSTAND THE *HELLER* CASE

In 2008, the Court decided a case called *District of Columbia v. Heller*.[20] The *Heller* opinion is often referred to as a "landmark" decision for gun rights advocates. The *Heller* case is important, because for the first time since 1939, the Supreme Court issued a direct ruling on how to interpret the meaning of the Second Amendment.

Prior to the decision in the *Heller* case, gun control advocates argued that the Second Amendment only protected the right to keep and bear arms for the collective members of a militia or the military. The United States Supreme Court decided in the *Heller* case that the right to keep and bear arms is an individual right that protects the right of individual citizens to keep and bear arms for self-defense purposes.

The *Heller* case was filed in 2003 by six plaintiffs, none of whom had a direct connection to the military. The plaintiffs challenged the Washington D.C. Handgun Ban in effect at the time, because the law prevented them from lawfully possessing a handgun in their homes. The first court to hear the case dismissed it, finding that the Second Amendment did not protect an individual's right to bear arms unless that individual was in service with a militia. The six plaintiffs appealed to the first tier of federal courts. That appellate court reversed the lower court's decision, and held that the ban was in fact unconstitutional. The case was then appealed to the United States Supreme Court by Washington D.C.

The United States Supreme Court decided that:

It is no answer to say, as petitioners[21] do, that it is permissible to ban the possession of handguns so long as the possession of other firearms (i.e. long guns) is allowed. It is enough to note, as we have observed, that the American people have considered the handgun to be the quintessential self-defense weapon. There are many reasons that a citizen may prefer a handgun for home defense: It is easier to store in a location that is readily accessible in an emergency; it cannot easily be redirected or wrestled away by an attacker; it is easier to use for those without the upper-body strength to lift and aim a long gun; it can be pointed at a burglar with one hand while the other hand dials the police. Whatever the reason, handguns are the most popular weapon chosen by Americans for self-defense in the home, and a complete prohibition of their use is invalid . . ."[22]

> In *Heller*, the Supreme Court decided that the Washington D.C. Handgun Ban was unconstitutional because it violated a right guaranteed by the Second Amendment—to own a handgun for self-defense in one's home.

After a thorough review of the history of the Second Amendment,[23] which takes into account the intent of the

Framers, the Court ruled for the first time in history that the Second Amendment protects an individual's right to possess firearms, apart from any connection to a militia or the military. In addition, the Court found that the individual's right to possess a firearm is for traditionally lawful purposes, such as self-defense within the home.

But once again, the Court also made it clear that the Second Amendment's protection is not unlimited. Justice Scalia wrote:

> Like most rights, the right secured by the Second Amendment is not unlimited. From Blackstone through the 19th-century cases, commentators and courts routinely explained that the right was not a right to keep and carry any weapon whatsoever in any manner whatsoever and for whatever purpose. For example, the majority of the 19th-century courts to consider the question held that prohibitions on carrying concealed weapons were lawful under the Second Amendment or state analogues . . .
>
> We also recognize another important limitation on the right to keep and carry arms. Miller said, as we have explained, that the sorts of weapons protected were those "in common use at the time." We think that limitation is fairly supported by the historical tradition of prohibiting the carrying of "dangerous and unusual weapons."
>
> It may be objected that if weapons that are most useful in military service—M-16 rifles and the like—may be banned, then the Second Amendment

right is completely detached from the prefatory clause.[24] But as we have said, the conception of the militia at the time of the Second Amendment's ratification was the body of all citizens capable of military service, who would bring the sorts of lawful weapons that they possessed at home to militia duty. It may well be true today that a militia, to be as effective as militias in the 18th century, would require sophisticated arms that are highly unusual in society at large. Indeed, it may be true that no amount of small arms could be useful against modern-day bombers and tanks. But the fact that modern developments have limited the degree of fit between the prefatory clause and the protected right cannot change our interpretation of the right.[25]

Justice Scalia concluded the court's opinion with the following advice about restrictions on the Second Amendment:

We are aware of the problem of handgun violence in this country, and we take seriously the concerns raised by the many amici who believe that prohibition of handgun ownership is a solution. The Constitution leaves the District of Columbia a variety of tools for combating that problem, including some measures regulating handguns. But the enshrinement of constitu-

> **What this means to you, the individual gun owner, is that if a city passes a law restricting you from possessing a handgun, that law is unconstitutional because it violates the Second Amendment right of an individual to keep and bear arms for self-defense purposes.**

tional rights necessarily takes certain policy choices off the table. These include the absolute prohibition of handguns held and used for self-defense in the home. Undoubtedly, some think that the Second Amendment is outmoded in a society where our standing army is the pride of our Nation, where well-trained police forces provide personal security, and where gun violence is a serious problem. That is perhaps debatable, but what is not debatable is that it is not the role of this Court to pronounce the Second Amendment extinct.[26]

Only two years after the decision in the *Heller* case, the United States Supreme Court heard another Second Amendment case and issued another decision in favor of gun owners: *McDonald v. Chicago*.[27] The *McDonald* case was necessary because Washington D.C. is a federal enclave (a separate entity enclosed within a larger entity), so the *Heller* decision was arguably limited to only restraining the federal government. The case did not necessarily bind the individual states. A lawsuit challenging a state or local gun ban would be required to address that issue.

Within forty-eight hours of the Supreme Court's *Heller* decision, two lawsuits challenging the City of Chicago's handgun ban were filed. Handguns were banned in only a few places in the United States, and Chicago was one of them, with a ban very similar to the Washington D.C. gun ban.

In *McDonald*, five Supreme Court justices agreed (and four did not) that the Second Amendment provides Americans a fundamental right to bear arms that cannot be violated by state and local governments. The analysis by the justices explains that the protections of the Second Amendment are incorporated into the Bill of Rights by way of the 14th Amendment.

What this means to you, the individual gun owner, is that if a city passes a law restricting you from possessing a handgun, that law is unconstitutional because it violates the Second Amendment right of an individual to keep and bear arms for self-defense purposes. In other words, states and cities now cannot pass laws that violate the Supreme Court's decision in the *Heller* case. *McDonald* is the benchmark case that protects people to a greater degree from states passing restrictive gun laws. Thanks to *McDonald*, state legislatures are now limited to some degree (how much is yet to be determined) in how extensive their gun control laws can be. The government can no longer prevent people from keeping and bearing handguns for self-defense purposes in the home (the holding in the *Heller* case). While some state legislatures are passing laws that prohibit the possession of certain firearms (mostly certain types of rifles deemed "assault rifles"), they cannot successfully pass a law that bans all types of firearms or even all handguns, because such a law would violate the federal constitution as the justices in the *McDonald* case explained.

The case law after *Heller* and *McDonald* continues to evolve. Lower court cases across the country issue opinions that do not apply across the states, but only affect the citizenry in the deciding court's jurisdiction. These cases are still important for the people who live in those jurisdictions, and eventually, some of these cases will make their way to the United States Supreme Court.

An example of such a case arose in California over the San Diego County Sheriff's onerous policy against issuing concealed carry permits. The Ninth Circuit Court of Appeals held that California's ban on open carry, coupled with the San Diego Sheriff's policy essentially prohibiting concealed carry permits, violated a citizen's Second Amendment right to keep and bear arms *outside* the home.[28] The Ninth Circuit reasoned that when people cannot open carry and also cannot obtain a concealed carry permit, then they effectively cannot carry at all outside their homes. The Court ruled that such a law violates the protection of the Second Amendment. This question remains to be decided by the United States Supreme Court.

Eventually, more cases will make their way to the United States Supreme Court, and thereby become the law of the land instead of being limited to the jurisdiction where the case is decided. In the meantime, courts in different jurisdictions (state and federal) can make different decisions. A law may be ruled unconstitutional by one court, and a very similar law upheld as constitutional by another court. So once again, you need to understand the law as it pertains to the specific states and cities in which you live or may travel with a firearm. Where, how, and what type of firearms you can carry are some of the trickiest laws because these laws vary to large degrees from place to place.

14

How the ATF Evolved with the Gun Laws

The Bureau of Alcohol, Tobacco, Firearms, and Explosives (the ATF) is going the extra mile to win your enthusiasm. Check out the agency's internet K-9 page, portraying the playful side of the dogs responsible for sniffing out the next Boston Marathon bomber. You will be greeted by a cute and fluffy retriever holding an "ATF" ball. While you are there, click the link to go to the "Kids Page" with coloring pictures and word games. This reminder of your own family is just a click away from pages showing the grim truth of what can happen when firearms wind up in the hands of murderers and drug dealers. The message is clear: It is a wonderful world—but everything you deem precious could be taken away. The ATF wants you to believe its agents are here to help.

> By passing the National Firearms Act, our government officially allowed criminals to dictate the interpretation of the Second Amendment, and concurrently targeted the firearms possessed by responsible gun owners in a severely misguided effort at crime control.

Many gun owners loathe the ATF. Gun business owners fear they will fail to dot an "i" or cross a "t" and lose their livelihood. Gun owners unabashedly abhor the unrelenting infringement on our constitutional protections by our own government. Many gun owners fear they will accidentally commit a felony and face prosecution for their ignorance.

One of the ATF's Assistant Directors suggested to me that no one wants the bad guy to have the gun, or the terrorist to have the bomb, no matter what side you are on. If we can agree on that, then we are working together.

The problem, of course, is the law's ever-expanding definition of "bad guy" and what, exactly, constitutes "public safety." In the 1920s, public safety meant not allowing hard-working Americans to enjoy a beer at 5:00 o'clock. It was a tax on alcohol in 1789, rather than any criminal activity, that gave birth to the agency.

While prohibition ended in 1933, the National Firearms Act (NFA) passed Congress in 1934, implementing America's first tax on firearms and giving this "tax enforcement agency" another reason to exist. The National Firearms Act imposed an outrageous tax on gangsters' favorite firearms: machine guns, short-barreled shotguns, and suppressors (silencers).

Rather than expect the criminals to obey the law and register firearms (which no one actually expected would happen), Congress intended to remove these "weapons" from circulation amongst the citizenry by taxing them into infinity. If citizens cannot afford them, they cannot buy them.

> The American gun owner suffers from the affliction of so many laws, most have little, if any, comprehension of all the ways they can run afoul of the imbroglio that is America's gun law system.

If law abiding citizens cannot buy them, they cannot get into criminals' hands. Such was the logic of the government, anyway. By passing the National Firearms Act, our government officially allowed criminals to dictate the interpretation of the Second Amendment, and concurrently targeted the firearms possessed by responsible gun owners in a severely misguided effort at crime control.

Today, nothing sends chills down the backs of law-abiding gun owners quite like a federal law enforcement agency specifically trained to spot and apprehend people for violating firearms laws. This chill is not because these gun owners intend to commit crimes—it is because they do not. Hence, the term "law-abiding." Rather, the chill arises from a rational fear of the unknown.

As you are now aware from our prior chapters, firearms laws are not like speed limits where there are clear signs posted along the highway to tell you what the limitations are and when you might be facing a violation. Instead, gun owners are left largely to their own devices to sort through the many levels of federal, state, and local laws, as well as the ever-expanding interpretations of those laws by the ATF and judges (who have not always agreed on the correct interpretation of the laws).

The American gun owner suffers from the affliction of so many laws, most have little, if any, comprehension of all the ways they can run afoul of the imbroglio that is America's gun law system. And there is no cure for criminal conduct. Once you have violated the law, accidentally or not, you cannot simply undo the criminal behavior. In other words, you cannot give a gun back to the person who sold it to you in another state without using an FFL and make things ok. I have posed this question to ATF agents, who confirmed that there is no way to "undo" accidental criminal behavior and "make it right."

While those who are anti-gun have trouble understanding how a person could "accidentally" commit a crime, it is actually pretty easy to transgress in the world of gun laws and face
imprisonment or a hefty fine. The chapters on the Gun Control
Act and National Firearms Act describe in detail how difficult
these laws can be to decipher and provide specific examples of
how they can easily, and unknowingly, be violated.

The problem does not stop with simply having too many
laws. It is one task to decipher thousands and thousands of laws
that regulate firearms, many of which defy common sense. It
is a completely different task to have to battle the amorphous
beast that is the ever-changing American gun law system. The
courts are not alone in creating this issue. The ATF may decide
an issue one way one day, and decide it another way the next.

It is no wonder that when most people think about the
ATF, they think about rules, restrictions, enforcement of rules
against people who did not mean to break the law, and iron-
fisted enforcement of rules that make no sense.

If you have gotten the sense that the gun laws that apply
to individual gun owners is daunting, think about all the rules,
regulations, and penalties that apply to gun businesses.

Business owners who unintentionally violate the Gun
Control Act (the GCA) provide a prime example. As we will
discuss in more detail later, the GCA imposes stricter licensing and regulation on the firearms industry, establishes categories of firearms offenses, and prohibits the sale of firearms and
ammunition to felons and certain other prohibited persons.
This law prevents young soldiers who may sacrifice their lives

for our country from purchasing a handgun from a gun shop to defend their own families until they reach age 21. It also prevents a gun owner from transferring firearms across state lines without using a dealer. There is no exception for family. If you want to give a firearm to your brother who lives in another state, you must send it to an FFL in his state instead of handing it to him at the Christmas family dinner. If you don't, YOU have committed a felony . . . and so has he.

Gun owners frequently ask if ATF agents actually pursue such cases. The answer is, "It depends." Many times, either no one is the wiser or the ATF has more important things to do. However, I have been told by ATF agents that they will pursue cases against people who ignorantly violate the law.

History also tells us that the ATF has been known to go after the unsuspecting gun owner or gun business owner (see Chapter 26 on How the ATF Abused the Gun Control Act). Evidence of the ATF's abuse of the Gun Control Act supported the passage of the Firearm Owner's Protection Act in 1986. Compromises to the proposed new law led to some harsh outcomes for gun owners, such as the ban on transferring machine guns made after 1986 to civilians. This ban was passed, despite the fact that over 175,000 machine guns were registered with ATF at the time, and not a single one had been used in a crime.[29]

Under federal law, the federal government is not supposed to maintain a registry of gun owners. In fact, the FBI is required to destroy background check records for gun purchasers before the start of the next business day. The truth is, the federal government has several hundred million records of gun owners, including multiple sales reports, trace records, and the records of dealers who have gone out of business. This knowledge further adds to the nervous feelings harbored by gun owners about the ATF.

When I asked a former ATF Director of Industry Operations (DIO), for her opinion of the ATF's reputation, she explained that the "ATF has a difficult job. People are trying to do the right thing. Often, there is some type of misunderstanding about the laws."[30] This former DIO confirmed that people are "stuck on their own" to figure out how to correct gun law violation issues. Having sat through FFL licensing inspection meetings, I can confirm that it is impossible, in a few hours, for an agent to thoroughly review and educate new gun dealers on the law. They hit the highlights, ask if you have any questions (questions which most people will not know to ask), and check the boxes that they went over a particular law with you and that you had no questions about it.

This former DIO also recognized that based on her prior experience working for the ATF, very few people actually intend to break the laws, but there are too many rules and regulations, especially for dealers and manufacturers, to do things perfectly on a daily basis.

I entirely agree with this point. It has been my experience as both a prosecutor and a civil law attorney that most law-abiding gun owners run afoul of the law not because they defend themselves with deadly force, but because they violate a law they were unaware even existed. The gun laws affecting most gun owners every day are those that pertain to how a person can carry (open, concealed, loaded, unloaded), where they can carry (inside a private business building, inside a state government building, inside a federal government building), who can possess a firearm (age restrictions, state law restrictions, permitting restrictions), and how they can transfer a firearm (in state, across states, sale, inheritance) without committing an accidental felony.

Despite the failings and the negative media coverage of the ATF as a whole (recall Waco, Ruby Ridge, Operation Fast & Furious), the individual agents who process our NFA and FFL paperwork are usually kind, helpful, and even sometimes sympathetic human beings. Many of them are not even anti-gun. I know ATF agents who have served our country through military service, or who have even operated their own gun related businesses.

On a day to day basis, ATF agents are either processing paperwork and assisting FFLs (the "regulatory side) or investigating crimes (the law enforcement side), much like other law enforcement agencies. Agents on the regulatory side can be extremely helpful in attempting to assist with a federal gun related issue, including answering a dealer's questions on how to abide by the law. Similarly, the ATF's website is full of helpful information for gun owners and gun businesses—assuming you know which questions to ask and where to look for answers.

At the end of the day, the ATF is charged with public safety and helping gun owners and gun businesses comply with the laws. Many of the agents who work for the ATF try to do just that. However, the Department of Justice's direction to the agency, *a la* Operation Choke Point or Operation Fast & Furious, has recently left a growing section of the public disquieted by the motives, character, and actions of the ATF. The recent proposals for more gun control and the country's great divide on the protection to be afforded by the Second Amendment further enhances this distrust and keeps the pro-gun community on the defensive.

The enlightened gun owner must remember that it was not the ATF that passed the tax act in 1789, or the NFA in 1934, or the GCA in 1968. Congress did. While Congress also created the agency to collect taxes, the ATF is also supposed to now exist to protect Americans from violent criminals, including terrorists. If we could just agree on one more thing . . . what that little word "infringed" really means . . . we may gain an agency that could focus entirely on its intended purpose and protect the law abiding citizens from the true criminals.

15

PUNISHING THE CITIZENS FOR THE CRIMES OF THE MOB: HOW THE FIREARMS LAWS KEPT THE UNTOUCHABLES EMPLOYED

The two federal laws I most often see people violate (usually unknowingly) are the National Firearms Act and the Gun Control Act.

The National Firearms Act (NFA) regulates only certain types of firearms. Fully automatic weapons (full-autos), short-barreled shotguns (SBSs), short-barreled rifles (SBRs), and suppressors (silencers) are the most common. Because the NFA only regulates specific types of firearms, it only affects the individuals who own or possess NFA firearms, and does not apply to everyone else who owns other types of firearms.

The Gun Control Act (GCA) affects *all* gun owners. The GCA also regulates gun dealers and establishes a list of "prohibited persons"—individuals who cannot lawfully possess a firearm. We will now review both of these laws with emphasis on the areas where gun owners are most likely to violate them and commit an "accidental felony."

The National Firearms Act (NFA)

The anti-gun community insists that more gun control laws will protect innocent children and stop gun violence. But gun owners know those arguments fail because criminals do not obey the gun control laws. Only law-abiding citizens obey the laws.

As Professor John Lott has stated, "I would ask gun control advocates one question: name a single place in the entire world where murder rates fell after gun control laws were passed."[31]

The concept is simple. A law-abiding firearm owner will purchase a firearm legally and will strive to use it legally. Criminals usually obtain firearms illegally by stealing them

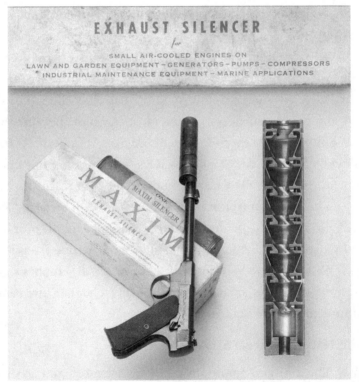

An original 1910 Maxim "Silencer," commonly sold in hardware stores and through the mail. Photo by Oleg Volk.

Silencers have not changed much over the last 100 years. A modern silencer, a Gemtech GM-22.

or buying them from other criminals because they can't buy them legally. Criminals then use illegal firearms to commit crimes, regardless of any law in place intended to prevent the crimes they commit.

In 2014, a criminal[32] in Santa Barbara, California, posted a YouTube video about how he hated women because they never shared any affection with him. He then stabbed his three roommates, shot three other people, and ran over four more people with his car. What followed was the typical ignorant cry for more gun control to stop the senseless killings. Yet, there was no cry for knife control or vehicle control or criminal behavior control. These killings occurred with legally obtained weapons—a lawfully purchased gun, a lawfully purchased knife, and a lawfully purchased vehicle.

By passing more gun control laws, the citizens the laws are "intended" to protect become disarmed and easy prey for the criminals who choose to disregard the laws.

Gun laws are not obeyed by criminals who are willing to take human life by committing murder.

This knowledge is not new. The federal government recognized the truth of the above statement when it enacted the first major federal gun control law on June 26, 1934: the National

79

Firearms Act (NFA). The NFA came after the St. Valentines Day Massacre in 1929 and the attempted assassination of President Roosevelt. The NFA is a registration system and excise tax (a separate tax applied to specific items or activities, such as a gasoline tax or a wagering tax) for certain types of firearms. It is also a pitfall for unsuspecting gun owners who can easily and unknowingly violate the NFA and commit an accidental felony.

The NFA is a gun control law written in a tax code. It is found in Title 26, United States Code section 5801 et. seq. (and the following pages). Title 26 is the Internal Revenue Code. The law is enforced by the Bureau of Alcohol, Tobacco, Firearms, and Explosives, formerly under the Department of the Treasury, but now overseen by the Department of Justice.

The NFA does not ban any firearms. The NFA was not passed to make criminals register firearms. The Attorney General knew criminals would NOT register firearms, and the original law did not require registration. Instead, the angle of this federal law was to tax law-abiding citizens who lawfully purchased certain firearms. The tax, at the time, was so high that many Americans could not afford to pay it. The law deterred these law-abiding citizens from purchasing the firearms subject to the NFA (which were the firearms being used by the gangsters). The law was a back route to reducing the number of those firearms that would be in circulation on the street. As with most gun control laws, the law-abiding citizens were and still are punished for the sins of the criminals.

The NFA requires that each time someone manufactures or transfers an NFA firearm, with few exceptions, the transferee is required to pay a $200 tax. A $200 tax is equivalent to a

$3,551.42 tax in 2015.[33]

Violation of the NFA carries criminal penalties. In other words, if you violate the NFA, you could be fined heavily and thrown in prison. A few ways you can violate the NFA include:

- Manufacturing or dealing in NFA firearms without paying the special occupational tax (SOT);

- Receiving or possessing *A "tax stamp" from the ATF.* illegally transferred or unregistered NFA firearms;

- Making an NFA firearm illegally (in other words, without getting prior permission from the ATF and paying the required tax) or making a false registration of an NFA firearm; or

- Obliterating, removing, changing or altering the serial number or identification required on an NFA firearm.

The penalties for these violations are up to 10 years in federal prison and up to a $250,000 fine. On top of these hefty penalties, any firearm, vessel, vehicle, or aircraft used to transport, conceal, or possess an NFA firearm involved in a violation of the NFA is subject to seizure and forfeiture.

The following is an exclusive list of what constitutes a "firearm" under the NFA:

1. **Short Barrel Shotgun (SBS)**: A shotgun having a smooth bore barrel or barrels of less than 18 inches in length; a weapon made from a shotgun if such weapon as modified has an overall

length of less than 26 inches or a barrel or barrels of less than 18 inches in length;

2. **Short Barrel Rifle (SBR)**: A rifle having a rifled barrel or barrels of less than 16 inches in length; a weapon made from a rifle if such weapon as modified has an overall length of less than 26 inches or a barrel or barrels of less than 16 inches in length;

3. **Any Other Weapon (AOW)**: This is a catch-all category. The AOW is defined as any weapon or device capable of being concealed on the person from which a shot can be discharged through the energy of an explosive. All ordinary pistols, revolvers, rifles, and shotguns are excluded and are not considered firearms. Examples of AOWs include gadget firearms such as pen guns, cane guns, and Ithaca auto-burglar guns, which fire a projectile by the action of an explosive. As we will see, this category also includes less obvious examples, which make this area of the law complex and a trap for the unwary;

4. **A Machinegun**: A firearm that fires multiple rounds with a single pull of the trigger. Included within the definition of machinegun is the frame or receiver of any such weapon, any part designed and intended solely and exclusively, or a combination of parts designed and intended, for use in converting a weapon into a machinegun.[34] This is an example of the law being non-intuitive—when a small part of a gun can be considered a "machinegun;"

5. **Any Silencer**: Silencers in the gun community are commonly referred to as suppressors, because they do not actually "silence" a firearm, but make it less audible;

6. **A Destructive Device**: These include explosive devices

like hand grenades, bombs, Molotov cocktails, anti-tank guns, and large caliber weapons like RPG launchers (bazookas) and mortars. "Large caliber" refers to any weapon having a barrel diameter of more than half an inch, so it would include calibers greater than .50 caliber. The ATF reclassified shotguns known as "streetsweepers" as destructive devices, giving owners until 2001 to register any they owned as NFA firearms or face applicable penalties under 26 U.S.C. Chapter 53.

If you are in doubt about the classification of a firearm, have the firearm inspected by a gunsmith. If you suspect a firearm is restricted under the NFA, you should consult with a knowledgeable firearms lawyer *without* transporting the firearm.

South African revolver shotgun, 12-gauge, now classified as a destructive device by the ATF (also known as a street sweeper). Photo by Oleg Volk.

Under federal law, you may legally acquire NFA firearms if you are not prohibited by federal, state, or local law from receiving or possessing firearms, AND you obtain prior approval from the ATF. Some states prohibit NFA firearms, or only allow certain ones. The NFA firearms you receive must be lawfully registered. If they are being manufactured, you must obtain prior approval from the ATF to have the NFA firearms made. To lawfully acquire any NFA firearms, you will need to complete an ATF form and submit a photograph, a set of fin-gerprints, and the signature of your chief law enforcement offi-cer (CLEO) with the completed form. In 2016, this law changed to only require that a CLEO receive a "notice." The Chief Law Enforcement Officer can be the Chief of Police, the County Sheriff, the head of the State Police, or even a District Attorney. The most common ATF forms are "Form 1," for use when man-ufacturing an NFA firearm, and "Form 4," for most transfers of NFA firearms. Form 1 can be uploaded and processed through the ATF's online portal, but Form 4 must currently be sent via the United States Postal Service and takes months for the ATF to return the "tax stamp."

Beware that a private citizen who owns an NFA firearm that is not registered cannot register the firearm and "make it good." Unregistered NFA firearms are contraband. The ATF advises anyone who is in possession of an unregistered NFA firearm to contact the nearest ATF office to arrange for its dis-position. If you are unsure of the registration status, contact the ATF to find out. Your contact must be in writing, and you must verify your identity. If your identity matches the identity of the registration, it will be confirmed. Firearm registration issues can often arise in estate proceedings when the owner of the firearms has died, and the family must address the registration and transfer of the firearms. A gun trust is an unbeatable asset for transferring firearms, and if drafted correctly, will avoid most, if not all, of the problems that may arise during estate proceedings.

Fostech origin 12 semi-automatic shotgun (an SBS). Photo by Oleg Volk.

Elite Tactical Systems 12 gauge shotgun (an SBS). Photo by Oleg Volk.

Custom Select Fire AR 15 po82 sample by Elite Tactical Systems (an SBR).
Photo by Oleg Volk.

The author with a Gemtech suppressed SBR. Photo by Josh Wolfe.

Elite Tactical Systems 12-gauge, Any Other Weapon (an AOW). Photo by Oleg Volk.

The author, firing an MP5K/PDW (a machine gun) with a Gemtech Multimount Suppressor. Photo by Gary Gelson.

1921, 1928, and 1938 Thompsons, 45ACP submachine guns. Photo by Oleg Volk.

M1 Thompsons (machine guns). Photo by Oleg Volk.

The author, firing a Gemtech suppressed Glock. Photo by Josh Wolfe.

The author, with her Gemtech suppressed FN FS 2000. Photo by Oleg Volk.

16

HOW CAN YOU UNKNOWINGLY VIOLATE THE NFA?

Is it a pistol, an SBR, or an AOW?

By applying the NFA to certain firearms with specific cosmetic features, we can see how easy it is to get confused and commit an "accidental felony." An analysis of what constitutes a pistol, SBR, and an AOW demonstrates this point:

If a firearm was originally designed as a rifle (to shoot from the shoulder), it will forever be a rifle and subject to the SBR barrel length analysis (if the barrel is 16 inches or less, or if the firearm's entire length is less than 26 inches, it is an SBR). This firearm can never be made into a pistol legally—once a rifle, always a rifle or a weapon made from a rifle.

Similarly, if the firearm was originally designed as a pistol, logic might dictate that it will always be a pistol. Not so. Think you own an ordinary pistol?

On the next page, the first image shows our original firearm that is less than 26 inches in overall length with a single grip and no stock. This firearm is, in fact, legally, a pistol,[37] *so long as* it was originally manufactured or transferred as a pistol.

If you take this ordinary pistol and add an *angled* foregrip, as in the next image, you legally still own a pistol.

National Firearm Act (NFA) Rules and Regulations:
Pistols, SBRs, & AOWs   ... as of 2015, as interpreted and enforced by the Bureau of Alcohol, Tobacco, & Firearms (ATF)

Gun with single grip and no stock.
Legally: **a Pistol**

*(27 CFR 478.11).
But: ATF requires that it have originally been
manufactured or transferred as a pistol.
Converting a rifle to a pistol is illegal.

Add an Angled Fore-Grip (AFG).
Legally: **Still a Pistol**

Add a bipod.   Legally: **Still a Pistol**

Add a Vertical
Fore-Grip (VFG).   Legally: An **"Any Other Weapon" (AOW)**

Because ATF classifies this as an NFA Title II item
the gun's receiver must first be registered as an AOW.
This requires payment of a **$5 tax** and ATF approval, which currently takes **10 months**.
Possession of an unregistered AOW is a felony punishable by 10 years in federal prison and up to $250,000 in fines.

Add a
full stock.   Legally: **A Short-Barreled Rifle (SBR)**

SBRs are also NFA Title II items.
The gun's receiver must be registered as an SBR.
This requires payment of a **$200 tax** and ATF approval, which currently takes **10 months**.
Possession of an unregistered SBR is a felony punishable by 10 years in federal prison and up to $250,000 in fines.

*Photo by
David
Bookstaber.*

92

Similarly, if you add a bipod, as in the third image, you again, legally still own a pistol.

If you add a *vertical* fore-grip, as in the fourth image, you have suddenly manufactured a firearm subject to the National Firearms Act—which is subject to enforcement by the ATF—which exposes the accidental transgressor (you) to federal felony punishments. You now own a firearm known as an "any other weapon" or "AOW," and, because the firearm is now subject to the NFA, the gun's receiver must first be registered as an AOW. Registration requires payment of a $5 tax and ATF approval. Possession of an unregistered AOW is a felony punishable by 10 years in federal prison and up to $250,000 in fines.

If you take the same pistol, but add a full stock to it so it is now "designed to shoot from the shoulder," as in the final image, you have unlawfully manufactured a short-barreled rifle (an SBR). SBRs are NFA firearms as well. The SBR's receiver must be registered as an SBR, a $200 tax must be paid, and ATF approval must be received before the rifle is manufactured. Possession of an unregistered SBR is also a felony punishable by 10 years in federal prison and up to $250,000 in fines.

The controlling analysis of the above AR style pistol focuses not only on what "furniture," such as bipods, grips, and stocks are added, but also on the firearm's "receiver." A "receiver" is the part of the firearm that houses all the required components to make the firearm work. Without the receiver, the firearm is inoperable. Many people are familiar with AR style rifles such as the AR-15 or the M16. These rifles have an "upper" and a "lower" receiver. It is the lower receiver that is required to be serialized and is considered by itself to be a firearm under federal law. The analysis of pistol versus rifle therefore begins with whether the firearm was designed with a lower receiver (sometimes just called a "lower") that was originally a pistol (not designated as a rifle) when it was first created.

Another hot topic is the "Sig Brace," shown in the next photographs. Wrap it around your forearm for stability, and you have an ordinary pistol. Use it to shoot from your shoulder, and you may have an SBR, according to the ATF.

These are only a few of the ways gun owners can accidentally violate the NFA.

How the Sig Brace is designed for use (lawful). Photo by Oleg Volk.

How the Sig Brace is actually used (unlawful unless registered with the ATF). Photo by Oleg Volk.

17

WHY IT'S EASY TO OWN A MACHINE GUN AND NOT KNOW IT

A machine gun. A DIAS is a small toggle device which, when installed in an AR type rifle, along with a few other parts, can convert a semi-automatic AR into a fully automatic rifle. Photo by Wally at York Arms.

Think you know whether you possess a machine gun? Did you know that Congress changed the definition of what constitutes a "machine gun" when it passed the Firearm Owners Protection Act (FOPA) in 1986? Since then, you own a machine gun if you simply own a part "designed and intended solely and exclusively" to convert a weapon into a machinegun. This has come as a shock to gun owners who have been greeted by ATF agents asking to collect their "machine guns."

Until the 1980s, it was fairly common to purchase a part known as a drop-in auto sear (DIAS). When a DIAS is installed into certain AR-15 style rifles with M16 internal components, it will convert the semi-automatic rifle into a fully-automatic rifle. Up until 1998, the ATF's position was that any DIAS man-

ufactured before 1981 was not subject to the NFA. In 1998, however, a federal judge decided that the ATF does not have the
authority to make such an exception to the law, and that all
firearms dealers "would do well to assume" that any transfers
of DIASs are subject to the NFA, regardless of when they were
manufactured and regardless of any supposed exceptions made
by the ATF.[38]

In short, another easy way for gun owners to violate the
NFA is to own certain parts of an NFA firearm and not register
those parts. The DIAS issue is a classic example of how the ATF
and the court deciding a case may not agree, to the detriment of
the unsuspecting gun owner. Let's examine how this can happen in more detail.

Prior to 1981, it was legal to possess a DIAS *unless* you
installed it, along with at least three other parts capable of converting a semi-automatic firearm into a fully-automatic firearm, without first obtaining ATF approval. On November 1,
1981, the ATF issued Ruling 81-4, an ATF agency ruling declaring that a DIAS by itself would now be included within the definition of machinegun, because the DIAS was "a combination
of parts designed and intended for use in converting a weapon
to shoot automatically more than one shot."[39] However, in the
same Ruling, the ATF also declared that Ruling 81-4 would
not be applied to auto-sears manufactured before November
1, 1981. In other words, pre-November 1, 1981, manufactured
auto-sears could be legally possessed as long as the possessor
did not also possess either an AR type rifle into which the DIAS
could be installed, or the other necessary M16 conversion parts.

Auto sears continued to be sold through various firearms

publications and on-line auction sites for the next 30 years. These DIASs were often advertised as "Pre-81 Drop-In Auto-Sears" and sold to unsuspecting members of the public.

1910 Maxim machine gun on a wheeled mount.
An obvious machine gun. Photo by Oleg Volk.

A DIAS installed.
A not-so-obvious machine gun. Photo by Wally at York Arms.

99

Another view of an installed DIAS. Photo by Wally at York Arms.

In 1986, Congress changed the definition of "machine gun" to its current definition when it enacted the Firearm Owners Protection Act (FOPA). The current language in the definition of "machinegun,"[40] referring to "any part designed and intended solely and exclusively . . . for use in converting a weapon into a machinegun" was not part of the definition in 1981, when the ruling was made. That additional language was added in 1986, as part of the FOPA amendments. The FOPA also forbade the future civilian transfer of any machinegun manufactured after May 19, 1986.

The enactment of the FOPA in 1986 means that possession of an auto-sear by itself is now a federal crime. The Seventh Circuit Court of Appeals has rendered an important decision on pre-1981 AR-15 drop-in auto sears.[41] The court indicated that such sears are not "grandfathered" as the ATF had been representing, and as owners of such items had believed. The court

100

ruled that it is, in fact, illegal to transfer or possess these sears, even if they were made before November 1, 1981. Because this case was decided by a lower federal court and not the United States Supreme Court, its decision is only binding to the lower courts within its own district. However, its decision could be persuasive enough that courts from other districts may choose to follow it.

The ATF continues to knock on doors and collect the pre-1981 auto-sears previously thought to be legal. I have been involved in this process. So far, none of my clients have been prosecuted, and the ATF agents have advised that they just want to collect the parts. However, as shown by the case mentioned above, people have been prosecuted for possession or transfer of auto-sears, and appellate courts in some jurisdictions have upheld such convictions.

If you possess an unregistered DIAS, it is a federal offense with criminal penalties (severe fines and prison time) to continue to possess it, and your only option as a law-abiding citizen is to allow the ATF to confiscate it. You will not be compensated for the part.

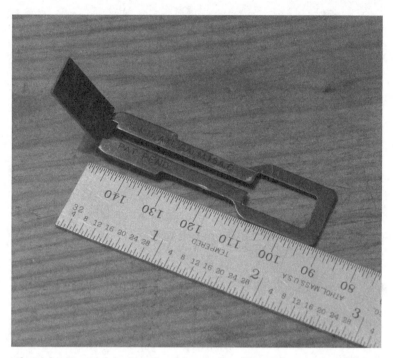

The Lightening Link is also a "machine gun," and is another way to easily convert a semi-automatic firearm into a fully automatic firearm. Photo by Wally at York Arms.

18

POSSESSING, TRAVELING, AND MOVING WITH NFA FIREARMS

Recall our discussion of "possession" in Section I. If you purchase an NFA firearm in your name, you are the only person authorized to be in "possession" of the firearm. For example, you cannot leave your silencer at home with your spouse, unless it is in a safe to which your spouse does not have the combination (you may have trouble selling that one to law enforcement or a jury).

If you wish to travel with your NFA firearms, and your travel will include crossing state lines, you may be able to take your NFA firearms with you. In order to do so lawfully, you will need the ATF's permission by submitting ATF "Form 20" before you travel across state lines. There is an exception for temporary travel with a suppressor or AOW, which are excepted from this rule, although ATF highly recommends Form 20 for all NFA firearms. Permission can be obtained from the ATF by submitting a letter containing all necessary information, or by submitting ATF Form 20 to the ATF, NFA Branch. Form 20 can take weeks (or longer) for the ATF to process.

If you move to a new state and your new state of residency does not allow possession of your NFA firearms, the ATF advises that you may leave your NFA firearms in a safe deposit

box (do they make them that big?) or store them in your former state in a friend's or relative's house in a locked room or
container to which only you have the key. If you choose this
option, you should make sure that the owner of the house
where you keep your firearms has a copy of the ATF "tax stamp"
paperwork showing to whom the firearms are registered, and
a signed letter from you authorizing storage of the firearms at
their residence.

19

WHY CAN CRAZY PEOPLE GET A GUN? THE PUBLIC OUTCRY THAT SPAWNED THE GUN CONTROL ACT OF 1968 (THE GCA)

The Gun Control Act of 1968, found under the United States Criminal Code,[42] was enacted after the assassinations of John F. Kennedy, Malcolm X, Robert F. Kennedy and Martin Luther King, Jr. It was signed into law by President Lyndon B. Johnson on October 22, 1968, after Congress declared:

> That the purpose of this title is to provide support to federal, state, and local law enforcement officials in their fight against crime and violence, and it is not the purpose of this title to place any undue or unnecessary federal restrictions or burdens on law-abiding citizens with respect to the acquisition, possession, or use of firearms appropriate to the purpose of hunting, trapshooting, target shooting, personal protection, or any other lawful activity, and that this title is not intended to discourage or eliminate the private ownership or use of firearms by law abiding citizens for lawful purposes, or provide for the imposition by Federal regulations of any procedures or requirements other than those reasonably neces-

sary to implement and effectuate the provisions of this title.[43]

The law is labeled the "State Firearms Control Assistance Act," but it is most commonly referred to as the "Gun Control Act" or the GCA.

In passing this law, Congress invoked the "Commerce Clause"[44] of the U.S. Constitution, targeting the regulation of interstate commerce in firearms. In other words, when guns or gun parts are sold across state lines, the crossing effectuates interstate commerce. Congress decided that it had the authority to create this law and impose restrictions on the transfer of firearms because almost all firearms (or their parts) are sold across state lines and affect interstate commerce.

The GCA sets forth the minimum restrictions that all states must follow, including the following key restrictions (as amended or updated by subsequent laws):

- Defines what constitutes a "firearm" subject to the GCA's restrictions;
- Requires dealers and manufacturers to obtain a federal firearms license (FFL);
- Places restrictions on how firearms may be transferred across state lines;
- Requires NICS (National Instant Criminal Background Check System) background checks whenever someone buys a firearm from an FFL;
- Generally prohibits interstate firearms transfers unless an FFL serves as an intermediary;
- Prohibits certain classes of individuals from possessing firearms;

- Prohibits the direct mail order of firearms by individuals;
- Prohibits individuals from purchasing handguns in a state where they do not reside;
- Imposes age restrictions for the transfer of firearms and ammunition by FFLs to individuals.

"Firearm" Defined in the GCA

The word "firearm" is specifically defined in the GCA, and the GCA's definition of firearm can be different from those in your own state's laws and from other federal laws. A "firearm" under the GCA is:

- Any weapon (including a starter gun) which will or is designed to or may readily be converted to expel a projectile by the action of an explosive;
- The frame or receiver of any such weapon;
- Any firearm muffler or firearm silencer; or
- Any destructive device.

Such term does not include an antique firearm.

Note that "antique firearms" are excluded from the definition of firearm. An antique firearm is

(A) Any firearm (including any firearm with a matchlock, flintlock, percussion cap, or similar type of ignition system) manufactured in or before 1898; or

(B) Any replica of any firearm described in subparagraph (A) if such replica

(i) is not designed or redesigned for using rimfire or conventional centerfire fixed ammunition, or

(ii) uses rimfire or conventional centerfire fixed

ammunition which is no longer manufactured in the United States and which is not readily available in the ordinary channels of commercial trade; or

(C) Any muzzleloading rifle, muzzleloading shotgun, or muzzleloading pistol, which is designed to use black powder, or a black powder substitute, and which cannot use fixed ammunition. For purposes of this subparagraph, the term "antique firearm" shall not include any weapon which incorporates a firearm frame or receiver, any firearm which is converted into a muzzleloading weapon, or any muzzleloading weapon which can be readily converted to fire fixed ammunition by replacing the barrel, bolt, breech-block, or any combination thereof.

Have you ever wondered why you can still mail order a muzzleloading rifle? The answer is that muzzleloading rifles are

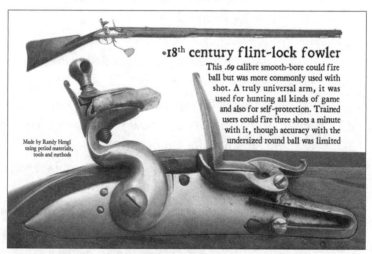

Not a firearm under the GCA. Photo by Oleg Volk.

"antiques" and not "firearms" under the definition of firearm in
the Gun Control Act. Because they are not considered firearms
by the GCA, muzzleloading rifles are not subject to the restrictions on mail orders found in the GCA.

Note, however, that states can pass more restrictive laws
so long as those laws do not violate the Second Amendment.
Therefore, muzzleloaders may still be considered "firearms"
under your state's laws.

*A reproduction flintlock rifle. Not
considered a firearm under the GCA.
Photo by Oleg Volk.*

20

Do You Need a Federal Firearms License (FFL)?

One of the primary stated purposes of the GCA is to prevent firearms from getting into the hands of criminals. The underlying premise of the law is that certain people should not own firearms.

To control who may or may not possess or purchase a firearm, the GCA created a police force through a permitting process: A federal firearms license (FFL) is required in order to be a dealer, manufacturer, or importer of firearms. These federal firearms licensees (FFLs) became responsible for ensuring that any firearm from their shop is never transferred to a "prohibited person," and that handguns are not transferred to someone who is a resident of a state different from the state in which the FFL conducts business. The ATF oversees the licensing process, and its agents regulate firearms businesses and investigate misconduct.

There are several categories of FFLs:

1. A "manufacturer" is a person who "devotes time, attention, and labor to manufacturing" firearms or ammunition, and the manufacturing occurs "in the regular course of trade or business with the principal objective of livelihood and profit through the sale or

distribution" of the firearms or ammunition that are manufactured.[45]

2. A "dealer" is any person who "devotes time, attention, and labor to dealing in firearms as a regular course of trade or business with the principal objective of obtaining livelihood through the repetitive purchase and resale of firearms."[46]

3. A "gunsmith" is a person who "devotes time, attention, and labor to engaging in such activity as a regular course of trade or business with the principal objective of livelihood and profit."[47]

4. A "pawnbroker" is a person "whose business or occupation includes the taking or receiving by way of pledge or pawn, of any firearm as security for the payment or repayment of money."[48]

5. An "importer" is a person who "devotes time, attention, and labor to importing firearms (or ammunition) as a regular course of trade or business with the principal objective of livelihood and profit through the sale or distribution" of the imported firearms or ammunition.[49]

The key element in determining whether someone needs an FFL is whether the person selling, manufacturing, or importing has the "principal objective of livelihood and profit." This definition looks to the person's intent—are you intending to make a living and financial gain from the sales, manufacture, or import, or are you just trying to improve or liquidate your personal collection? The ATF analyzes whether a license is required on a case by case basis. Making (or losing) money does not by itself define your intent. Also, there is no minimum number of firearms that must be sold to be "engaged in business." In other words, you cannot determine that you do not need a license simply because you only sell five guns (for example) per year.

Instead, the ATF will look at a number of factors together to determine whether someone is engaged in a firearms or ammunition business. The factors the ATF analyzes include 1) the quantity of firearms or ammunition you are moving; 2) the frequency of the transactions; 3) your intent; and 4) your representations to the buyer about your ability and willingness to obtain or transfer firearms. Whether or not someone should have an FFL is to a certain degree left open to interpretation. For this reason, some people who occasionally sell or repair firearms will obtain an FFL to ensure they are operating within the law. The ATF recommends that if you are not sure whether you need a license that you contact your local ATF office to discuss your situation and allow them to help you evaluate the facts of your case.

It is not unusual for gun owners to resell firearms. Some individuals even regularly buy and sell, including doing so at gun shows. The GCA carves out exceptions to the licensing requirement for people who may occasionally sell or improve firearms, even at gun shows. The exceptions are for people who make "occasional sales, exchanges, or purchases of firearms for the enhancement of a personal collection or for a hobby," or people who sell "all or part of [a] personal collection of firearms"[50] or who make "occasional repairs" or who occasionally fit "special barrels, stocks, or trigger mechanisms to firearms."[51]

If any of these exceptions apply, the person is not considered to be "engaged in the business" and is not required to obtain a license. In the current political climate, extreme caution is warranted. The ATF has been investigating gun owners who regularly buy and sell firearms, including at gun shows, in an effort to close the so-called "gun show loophole." The "gun show loophole" is a phrase tossed around by gun prohibitionists to reference the lack of background checks performed when sales occur between private parties. Note that the ATF is investigating gun owners for buying and selling at gun shows, even though the ATF's own application for a federal firearms license (Form 7) specifically states that gun owners who are *only* buying and selling at gun shows may not submit an application for a license. Don't take the risk—if you regularly buy and sell, talk to the ATF or a firearms attorney to make sure you do not need a license.

You are allowed to make your own firearms for your personal use, so long as the firearms are not for sale or distribution and so long as you are not prohibited from possessing a firearm. But there are exceptions to this general rule. For example, you are not allowed to assemble a non-sporting or semiautomatic rifle from 10 or more imported parts.[52] Also, if you wish to create an NFA firearm, you must first pay the required tax, and file and receive an approved ATF Form 1. Note that unless you are making your own NFA firearm, you do not need to mark the firearm. However, the ATF recommends you mark the firearm with a serial number or other identification marks to assist law enforcement with the recovery of the firearm in the event it is stolen or lost.

In order to acquire an FFL, you must meet certain requirements. Some of these requirements mimic the GCA provisions about who can or cannot possess a firearm.

An FFL:

1. Must be at least 21 years of age;

2. Cannot have been convicted of a crime punishable by imprisonment for a term exceeding one year; is not a fugitive, an unlawful user of or addicted to a "controlled substance," an illegal alien, a person adjudicated mentally defective or who has been committed to a mental institution, a person who has renounced U.S. citizenship or who has been discharged from the Armed Forces under dishonorable conditions, and cannot be subject to a court order restraining him or her from harassing, stalking, or threatening an intimate partner or child of such partner;

3. Has not willfully violated any federal firearms laws or regulations;

4. Has not willfully withheld or failed to disclose any information required, or has not made any false statement in the application;

5. Has premises from which he conducts or intends to conduct business (can be a business or home as long as it is a permanent structure). The business must be open to the clientele designated by the licensee to be served; and

6. Must comply with all state and local laws (including local zoning ordinances).

A person who wishes to obtain an FFL must submit ATF Form 7 to the ATF regional office, the correct fee for the license the person seeks, photographs, and fingerprints obtained from a law enforcement agency. The ATF has 60 days to approve or reject the application. Information on how to apply is available at **http://www.atf.gov/firearms/how-to-become-an-ffl.html**. Your state may have additional licensing procedures, so be sure to check with your state's Attorney General's office to find out if you must submit a separate state application.

The federal government imposes a special "tax" called the Special Occupation Tax (SOT) for licensees whose businesses include NFA firearms. Fees differ for licensees who will be working with NFA firearms, destructive devices, or simply collecting curios and relics.

There are many rules that apply to FFLs, such as how to keep records of their business transactions. FFLs must keep clear records of the firearms they receive, including when they receive and dispose of them—known as "acquisitions and dispositions" or "A&D." The law imposes strict timelines for FFLs to record this information. FFLs must also ensure that all transferees may lawfully possess firearms. FFLs, not the government, are supposed to keep their transfer records (Form 4473). However, when an FFL goes out of business, their records are transferred to the ATF. The federal government has several hundred million records from FFLs who close their doors.[53] They also legally collect other required FFL "forms," such as "multiple handgun sales" and reports and information about lost or stolen firearms.

FFLs must strictly follow these rules, and their records are subject to an annual "compliance review" by ATF agents who could show up anytime during business hours, or in the course of a criminal investigation. If an FFL has made any record-keeping mistakes, those mistakes are recorded in a "Report of Violations." Depending on the types of violations and how many, the FFL may be subject to disciplinary action. This disciplinary action can range from a warning letter to a notice that the ATF will revoke the FFL's license.

My preference is to help business owners avoid ever having violations. To do so, we provide FFLs with on-site visits, additional assistance and checklists to avoid the most common mistakes. Unfortunately, some clients make their first call to my office when there is a problem, such as the dreaded license revocation proceeding. While I have successfully battled the ATF to protect my client's license, these cases can be difficult to win. One reason for this difficulty is that the ATF does not usually attempt to revoke a license unless the FFL's violations are severe and repetitive. To make matters worse, the ATF acts as prosecutor, judge, and jury at the hearings. If a hearing is lost, the FFL must file a court action and appeal the decision of the ATF. It is unlikely that an FFL will succeed in court because courts generally defer to the government agency's expertise.

The lesson here is that obtaining your FFL is serious business. Once you are an FFL, you have a host of new laws with which you must comply. Failure to comply with these additional laws can result in both the loss of your license AND criminal prosecution. It is essential that an FFL obtain the services of a qualified firearms attorney.

21

WON'T PEOPLE SUE ME FOR SELLING IMPLEMENTS OF DEATH IF I'M A DEALER OR MANUFACTURER?

There is no doubt that firearms manufacturers come under fire after mass shootings. Victims' families and the general population look for someone to blame, other than the criminal, who is actually to blame. Although this phenomenon is in and of itself mildly conversation-worthy, it is more interesting that Congress passed a law in 2005 to protect firearms dealers and manufacturers from this type of "negligence" lawsuit.

The Protection of Lawful Commerce in Arms Act of 2005 (PLCAA) is a law that requires that a lawsuit must be thrown out if the person filing the lawsuit claims the manufacturer or dealer was "negligent" in manufacturing a firearm because firearms can kill other people. Manufacturers and dealers can still be held liable for defective products, breach of contract, criminal misconduct, or other violations of the law.

You may be thinking that many other products pose a similar risk of injury to other people. Similar laws protect manufacturers of automobiles, power tools, and other "dangerous" products from overzealous plaintiffs looking for someone to blame for the actions of an individual. Unfortunately, prior to the PLCAA's enactment, some firearms dealers and manufacturers had been successfully sued for "negligence" by the mere act of producing and distributing firearms to the public.

Of course, the PLCAA does not always stop gun control advocates from trying to punish firearms manufacturers. After the 2012 Sandy Hook school shooting, the victims' families attempted to sue Bushmaster Firearms International LLC.[54] These plaintiffs alleged that Bushmaster was negligent in producing and distributing the AR-15 rifle to a populace who is not trained to use it and would not understand its power. They claimed that Bushmaster should have foreseen that someone would misuse such a rifle, because it poses an unreasonable and egregious risk of injury to other people. In a similar suit after the Aurora Theater shootings in Colorado, plaintiffs sued the online ammunition manufacturer. The federal judge deciding the Aurora Theater case not only threw it out, but also ordered that the plaintiffs pay the legal fees of the company they sued. While these lawsuits were rightfully tossed to the curb, gun control advocates continue to advocate for the repeal of the PLCAA.

22

BANNED: YOU MAY NOT HAVE A GUN!

Certain categories of people cannot lawfully possess a gun. Gun owners can unintentionally run afoul of this law either by transferring (which includes selling) a firearm to someone on the prohibited person list, or by allowing a prohibited person to "possess" a firearm simply by being in their home. Remember, "possess" can mean simply being near a firearm and having the opportunity to exercise control over that firearm—it does not necessarily mean ownership or even physical contact with the firearm. Violating this law does not result in a slap on the wrist. It is a crime. Dealers and non-dealers alike cannot sell or transfer to people on the prohibited persons list, and prohibited persons cannot possess a firearm at all—even if they acquire it through gift or inheritance.

The Gun Control Act's list of "prohibited persons" includes any person:

- Under indictment or information in any court for a crime punishable by imprisonment for a term exceeding one year;
- Convicted of a crime punishable by imprisonment for a term exceeding one year;
- Who is a fugitive from justice;

- Who is an unlawful user of or addicted to any controlled substance;
- Who has been adjudicated as a mental defective or has been committed to any mental institution;
- Who is an illegal alien;
- Who has been discharged from the military under dishonorable conditions;
- Who has renounced his or her United States citizenship;
- Who is subject to a court order restraining the person from harassing, stalking, or threatening an intimate partner or child of the intimate partner; or
- Who has been convicted of a misdemeanor crime of domestic violence.

The GCA also restricts possession of handguns by minors. You must be 18 to possess a handgun, but you have to be over 21 to purchase one from an FFL. The GCA provides exceptions to these rules for employment, target practice, education, and a handgun possessed while defending one's own home. I discuss laws related to minors in more detail in the chapter titled Kids, Guns, and the Law.

Most of the categories of people who cannot have a gun are self-explanatory, but there are pitfalls. Here are a few to watch out for:

1. **"Convicted" of a felony or misdemeanor crime of domestic violence.** Whether or not someone is "convicted" of a crime depends on how the applicable laws define "conviction." The applicable law will be either federal or state, depending on whether the person was convicted of a federal crime (such as defrauding the IRS) or

a state crime (such as the felonies of murder or rape or a misdemeanor crime of domestic violence). Note that if the accused receives a withheld judgment or deferred sentence, but pleads guilty in order to do so, they are deemed "convicted" until the case is dismissed through another process. The law of the state or federal government will then determine whether or not the person can restore their rights by expungement, pardon, or some other process.

State laws vary as to whether a person is "convicted" of a crime. The word "conviction" depends on the state laws in which the conviction was entered, because those laws will define what measures, if any, that state allows to restore rights to the convicted person. In other words, the state laws that took the person's rights away also determine how the person can get the rights reinstated.

Some states automatically reinstate gun ownership rights upon completion of a sentence for certain crimes. Other states have application processes, such as expungement, withheld judgments, and pardons. These options are not mutually exclusive. Some states allow for any one or all of these scenarios. All three processes are designed to erase a conviction from a person's record or reduce the severity of the crime. How gun rights may be restored after they have been lost is affected by the conviction as well as these legal methods of reducing or eliminating convictions from the record.

Under the federal system, some crimes are excluded from the definition of a "felon." In other words, if you are convicted of certain federal felonies, they "don't count" as convictions, and they will not affect your gun rights. These excluded offenses include federal or state offenses pertaining to antitrust violations, unfair trade practices, restraints of trade, or other similar offenses relating to the regulation of business practices as well as state misdemeanors that carry a term of imprisonment of two years or less. If this list does not seem clear to you, you are not alone. The meaning of these categories is still being decided by the courts. For example, one court found that rolling back vehicle odometers was an "unfair trade practice" so the felony conviction in that case did not affect the defendant's gun rights.[55]

Whether someone is "convicted" also depends on the state where the person resides. This is because not all states accept the pardons or similar processes of other states. As a result, someone might be "convicted" in one state and "not convicted" in another. For example, a person might have received a pardon in one state, but the state in which they live now will not recognize the pardon from the other state. In that situation, the state law where the person lives will control, because the would-be gun owner will fail a background check when attempting to purchase a gun. This non-recognition of another state's process may very well be unconstitutional, but to date, remains unchallenged. The gay marriage issue serves as a good analogy: homosexuals argued that a state's law that did not recognize their valid marriage according to another state's laws was unconstitutional. In

2015, the United States Supreme Court agreed.[56] A similar argument needs to make its way to the Supreme Court regarding state laws that define whether a person remains convicted of a crime when the originating state declares that the person is no longer convicted.

2. Another area of confusion is the "unlawful user of or addicted to controlled substances" definition. According to the ATF, holders of state-issued medical marijuana cards are automatically "prohibited persons."[57] This position makes sense, because despite *state* laws legalizing marijuana, the *federal* government still considers marijuana a controlled substance. This means that federal agents can, if they wish, prosecute medical marijuana users for a violation of federal law, regardless of whether a state allows it. If someone does not give the government proof via an ID card that they are a controlled substance user, the government must prove that the person uses drugs "with regularity, over an extended period of time, and contemporaneously with the purchase or possession of a firearm."[58] In other words, one-time use of a drug should not effectively take a person's gun rights away. The key is a pattern of use that the government must prove.

3. Adjudicated a Mental Defective Includes More than the Mentally Ill. According to ATF regulations, the phrase "adjudicated a mental defective" means:

(a) A determination by a court, board, commission, or other lawful authority that a person, as a result of marked subnormal intelligence, or mental illness, incompetency, condition, or disease:

    (1) Is a danger to himself or to others; or

    (2) Lacks the mental capacity to contract or manage his own affairs.

(b) The term shall include:

    (1) A finding of insanity by a court in a criminal case; and

    (2) Those persons found incompetent to stand trial or found not guilty by reason of lack of mental responsibility pursuant to articles 50a and 72b of the Uniform Code of Military Justice, 10 U.S.C.A. sec 850a, 876b.[59]

This definition is, arguably, much broader than what Congress intended, given that the preface to the GCA indicates that the law was not intended to deprive law-abiding gun owners of their right to own firearms for hunting, sporting, or self-protection purposes. The result, however, of the broadened ATF definition, is that veterans and senior citizens are groups targeted by the federal government. I include special chapters on these two topics, because the current application of the law to these groups by governmental agencies is particularly atrocious.

We will see how someone who is on social security, or for whom a court has appointed a guardian or a conservator, loses their gun rights. This is an abhorrent scenario for war veterans who often simply need a little help readjusting, but lose their guns in the process.[60]

This prohibition also activates when parents attempt to gain control of a troubled teen through the court system. Many parents fail to consider and fully realize the long-term effect of this action. By asking a court to intervene, they may cause their child to be "adjudicated a mental defective," resulting in the child's loss of gun rights that carries into adulthood.

23

SENIORS, GUNS, AND THE SECOND AMENDMENT

Firearms-related issues for aging and incapacitated adults, whether due to declining mental health, physical health, or trauma, is an increasing dilemma. Many professionals who work with seniors in various capacities may have only a vague idea as to the issues involved, and their own, potential liability, if correct policies and procedures are not in place and strictly followed.[61]

Imagine that you are the court-appointed caretaker (commonly known as a guardian or conservator) for a war veteran who no longer remembers to pay his bills on time or take his medications. The veteran may be a relative or friend of yours, and is a gun owner. You are faced with the task of telling him that you are going to remove his guns from his home. You have to tell him this, because the phrase "adjudicated a mental defective" under federal law is defined as:

"A determination by a court, board, commission, or other lawful authority that a person, as a result of . . . incompetency, condition, or disease . . . lacks the mental capacity to contract or manage his own affairs."[62]

The elements of the above test encompass the standard in many states for how a state court can take away a person's

129

right to make decisions for himself, and appoint a guardian or conservator to make decisions for that person. Guardians and conservators are frequently appointed for seniors who are declining mentally or physically and who need the help of a friend, family member, or professional to pay their bills or assist them with other tasks of daily living. When such a court order exists, the person can no longer possess firearms under the Gun Control Act. On top of this inherently unsettling situation, the court-appointed caretaker could be held liable if the appointee shoots and kills another person or commits suicide with a firearm.

Friends, families, and professionals who care for senior citizens need to realize how court orders can affect seniors' gun rights. These caretakers should set aside any personal biases or unnecessary fears about firearms to help protect a person's Second Amendment rights while ensuring the protected person's safety. At the same time, these caretakers should also realize the criminal and civil liability that can accompany their roles as the responsible adults.

Caretakers who work with seniors should respect the senior's wishes when possible. Rights, including the right to defend oneself, should only be taken away from individuals when there is no other option to protect them or those around them—not because a caretaker or caretaker's company is averse to guns.

Lumping seniors into a category with the mentally ill, which is an entirely different topic,[63] is misleading and a disservice to senior gun owners. A gun may be the only equalizer in a self-defense situation for an elderly person living alone, so it is crucial that this subject be evaluated seriously and fairly. Many of my clients are seniors, and I routinely receive questions from them about when they can lawfully use deadly force to defend themselves against younger, stronger people. Again, a firearm is often the only equalizer in a disparity of force situation.

An elderly person's inability to balance a checkbook or remember to pay bills on time, along with other factors, can be cause for a court to appoint a conservator. A senior may also apply to the Social Security Administration to have a "representative payee" who will collect the senior's social security payments and communicate with the Social Security Administration. This issue incited media attention when the current presidential administration announced it was requesting the Social Security Administration to report those who use a representative payee to manage their social security income payments to the FBI. It may never cross the caretaker's mind that because a senior needs assistance with daily financial management that they are not allowed to possess a gun for personal protection.

The caretaker may also not realize that to "possess" does not necessarily mean "own." Possession can merely be the ability to access the firearms under the theory of law known as "constructive possession." If the guns are not locked up such that the protected person cannot get to them, the protected person and anyone who knowingly assists that person to be in possession or constructive possession is violating federal criminal law.

In comparison, if a senior has prepared for incapacity by creating a trust or power of attorney, there may not be a court process when they start to lose the capacity to care for themselves. Instead, their named agent or trustee may be able to begin managing their care and finances for them without the person being "adjudicated a mental defective." The key is to avoid the "adjudication." An "adjudication" is a formal decision, by a court or board, such as the Veterans Administration or the Social Security Administration. Of course, sometimes, for the safety of the senior and others, the guns must be removed from the home.

24
Veterans & the Veterans Administration

The Department of Veterans Affairs (the VA) regularly reports veterans it considers incompetent to the National Instant Criminal background Check System, which causes them to lose their gun rights. One of my primary practice areas is to help veterans who have lost their gun rights to get them back. I have seen the VA take a veteran's gun rights away simply because after serving this country, he needed long-term medical rehabilitation, which included multiple surgeries. Because this veteran did not reply to a VA form mailed to him that requested he tell the VA who would manage his finances while he was undergoing treatment, the VA declared him mentally incapacitated, appointed him an agent who would manage his finances, and reported him "adjudicated a mental defective" to the FBI. This VA action, of course, revoked the veteran's right to possess a firearm. Have no doubt, the VA regularly infringes upon veterans' gun rights.

In fact, the VA has declared that:

The Veterans Benefits Administration (VBA), through a Memorandum of Understanding with the Federal Bureau of Investigation (FBI), is providing the FBI with information on veterans rated as incompetent, incompetent surviving spouses, adult helpless children and dependent parents. Licensed gun dealers are required to check the NICS system to see if an individual is in a prohibited category before transferring a firearm to that individual. . . . Under the law, we are to routinely provide updated information on 'new' incompetents. If an individual previously rated incompetent has their competency restored, under the law they are still permanently restricted from purchasing or redeeming a firearm and information concerning that individual will not be stricken from the NICS index.[64]

You get the point of view of the VA: They prefer to keep guns away from veterans. Despite this memorandum by the VA about not restoring a veteran's rights, federal and state programs for the removal of disabilities do exist, and we address these options next.

25

RESTORING GUN RIGHTS

Whether or not a person who has lost the right to possess a firearm can restore that right depends on 1) why the right was lost and 2) under which laws (state or federal) the right was lost.

Some people do not even find out they have lost their gun rights until they try to buy a gun from an FFL. Imagine the shock and embarrassment of receiving a "denial" from the FBI at the gun shop. This scenario does not just happen to drug addicts and other criminals. It happens to seniors and to our veterans.

The first step in restoring the right to possess a firearm is to understand exactly why the right was lost. If you do not know, you can find out by submitting a request to the FBI to review the denial online.[65] At this website, you can give the transaction number (the number the dealer will give you when you are denied), input additional information, and attach documents.

Restoring rights is best accomplished by an attorney with the experience to know what to file and where to file it. Some restoration issues require court action while other issues can be cleared up by getting the correct records to the FBI. The process of restoring a person's gun rights is called obtaining "relief from disabilities."

Once you know why a person is prohibited from possessing a firearm, you can determine the correct course of action. Sometimes gun rights must be restored through a state process, other times they must be restored through a federal process, and still on other occasions, there is a combination of both state and federal processes instituted to restore an individual's rights.

Two of the most common reasons a person seeks relief from firearms disabilities are criminal convictions and having been adjudicated a mental defective.

As we discussed earlier, whether someone is convicted of a crime depends on the law of the state where they were convicted, or if they were convicted of a federal crime, the laws of the federal government. Whichever system is invoked, the restoration process used will depend primarily on the law of the jurisdiction that found the person "convicted."

States have various processes for removing a conviction from someone's record. The most common options are to file a motion to dismiss a withheld judgment or deferred sentencing agreement, to file a motion to expunge a record or to request a pardon. The time it will take to have a judge or board review your motion or application depends on the state system with which you are working. I have obtained a client's expungement within a couple of weeks, but I have also had to fight for a client's pardon for over three years. Every system is different. Again, hiring expert legal counsel to help you through the process can make the experience a positive one.

Those who have been convicted of a federal offense do not have all the options offered by state governments. Unless a federal conviction qualifies as one of the few excepted offenses (antitrust, restraint of trade, and unfair trade practices),[66] a federal felony conviction prohibits a person from obtaining, receiving, transporting, or possessing any firearm or ammunition for life. But, there are three theoretical opportunities for a person to restore their gun rights in the federal system.

The first possibility is a presidential pardon.[67] This option is not available until five years after release from custody or if there was no imprisonment, five years from the date of conviction. If the conviction is for tax, controlled substance, weapons, large fraud, public corruption, or violent crime offenses, there is a mandatory seven year waiting period. Pardons at both the state and federal level take time, because usually, the agency reviewing the request for a pardon will conduct a thorough investigation. Very few presidential pardons are granted.

The second possibility is a federal "expungement of a conviction." Unlike state expungement systems, there is no statutory expungement procedure written in the federal laws. Some courts have decided that they have the power to expunge a conviction, but practically speaking, expungements will not happen under the federal system.[68]

The third possibility is to apply for relief from the disability by submitting a form to the ATF.[69] In earlier years, approximately one-third of such applications were approved and gun rights restored to those applicants. The Attorney General is given the authority to grant this relief if, after reviewing the circumstances, "it is established to his satisfaction . . . that the applicant will not be likely to act in a manner dangerous to public safety and that the granting of the relief would not be contrary to the public interest."[70] The Attorney General does not directly review these applications. Instead, the Attorney General has delegated the investigation and enforcement of firearms laws to the Director of the Bureau of Alcohol, Tobacco, Firearms and Explosives.[71] However, since 1992, Congress has prohibited the ATF from processing such applications.[72] In other words, while a federal restoration of rights process technically exists, there is no money to make it work.

As a result, those convicted of a prohibiting federal felony have no viable option to restore their rights.

As for the mental adjudication restoration process, this is an area where Congress has held out the proverbial carrot to state governments to entice those governments to report more information to the FBI and to only restore rights to those who meet the federal government's criteria.[73] If a state has a program that meets the federal government's criteria, the FBI will update the person's record to reflect a cleared record. If the state's program does not meet the federal government's guidelines, there is no method to restore rights other than to resort to the court system.

Not too long ago, one brave person did just that.[74] Clifford Tyler filed suit against the government because he wished to restore his right to possess a firearm twenty-eight years after he had been committed to a mental institution. Mr. Tyler was so devastated when his wife of twenty-three years ran off with another man and depleted his finances, that his daughter called the police when he was crying and pounding his head on his kitchen floor. The police obtained a psychological evaluation, and thus began Mr. Tyler's involuntary commitment to a mental institution for his own safety. He stayed at the institution for less than a month. He had no violent or criminal past of any kind, and at the time the court reviewed his case, he was 73 years old.

In Mr. Tyler's case, the court reviewed the history of the federal relief from disabilities program and noted that Congress had defunded the program. The court also noted that only half the states have taken the Congressional carrot of grant money to implement a federally approved state relief from disabilities program. Because Mr. Tyler did not reside in one of the states with such a program, he had no way to restore his gun rights. The Court found that the portion of the Gun Control Act that prohibited Mr. Tyler from possessing a firearm violated the Second Amendment as it applied to Mr. Tyler.

The Court wrote that Mr. Tyler was caught in a catch-22: He could not obtain relief through the federal government due to lack of funding, and he could not obtain relief under a state program because his state had not implemented a relief program satisfactory to the federal government. The Court opinion states, "Under this scheme, whether Tyler may exercise his right to bear arms depends on whether his state of residence has chosen to accept the carrot of federal grant money and has implemented a relief program. His right thus would turn on whether his state has taken Congress's inducement to cooperate with federal authorities in order to avoid losing anti-crime funding. An individual's ability to exercise a 'fundamental righ[t] necessary to our system of ordered liberty,' *McDonald*, 561 U.S. at 778, cannot turn on such a distinction."[75] Mr. Tyler's case thus provides some hope to others who may be appropriate candidates for relief from firearms disabilities, but who find no process available to restore their rights.

Even when a person jumps through all the hoops to clean up their past and restore their right to possess a firearm, getting the FBI to update incorrect records is a process in itself. A good place to start is to upload the right documents and a request to correct records to the FBI using its online NICS appeal form mentioned at the beginning of this chapter. If that process is not satisfactory, hiring a lawyer to help is essential. When you hire a lawyer to help you through the process, the lawyer will ask you to sign the FBI's power of attorney form, so the law office can communicate directly with the FBI on your behalf. It is sometimes necessary for the lawyer to submit an additional appeal letter to the FBI, which clearly spells out why the FBI's records need to be corrected. If that process is unsuccessful, the lawyer can help you obtain relief through the court system.

With persistence, it is possible to reinstate lost gun rights under certain circumstances.

26

HOW THE ATF ABUSED THE GUN CONTROL ACT

After the enactment of the Gun Control Act, allegations arose that ATF agents, who were charged with enforcement of the GCA, abused the law. Rather than targeting criminals, the ATF agents were targeting law-abiding gun owners. The allegations against the ATF included that the agency repeatedly inspected FFL holders for the apparent purpose of harassment intended to drive the FFL holders out of business.

In response, the NRA pushed for reform, and Congress passed the Firearm Owners Protection Act (FOPA) in 1986.[77] This law, as most, wound up as a compromise.

The good, pro-gun amendments in the FOPA make it legal once again to sell long guns to non-residents of the state where an FFL conducts business, allow for the shipping of ammunition through the United States Postal Service, remove the record keeping requirements on non-armor piercing ammo, protect gun owners who transport firearms through

> A February 1982 report by a Senate subcommittee that studied Second Amendment issues found that 75% of ATF prosecutions "were aimed at ordinary citizens who had neither criminal intent nor knowledge, but were enticed by agents into unknowing technical violations."[76]

states where those firearms are prohibited (under certain conditions), limit the ATF's compliance inspections on FFLs to one per year, and forbid a federal registry linking non-National Firearms Act firearms to their owners.

With the good, also came some bad and ugly. The FOPA banned the sale of machineguns to civilians, except for machineguns that were manufactured prior to 1986. The cost of fully automatic weapons skyrocketed. With only so many guns available to be sold to civilians, the price of those guns increased accordingly. This part of the law passed despite the research by political scientist Earl Kruschke, whose research indicated that at the time, there were approximately 175,000 registered automatic firearms in circulation, and not a single one had been used in a crime.[78]

Despite the apparent protections the FOPA was supposed to provide, issues still arise for gun owners traveling interstate with their firearms, and there are still federal databases of gun owners and transactions.

A major "protection" of the Firearm Owner's Protection Act is to ensure that lawful gun owners receive safe passage through states with strict gun control laws. The FOPA allows safe passage if the traveler is just passing through that state with only short stops for food and gas, with firearms and ammunition that are not immediately accessible. Not immediately accessible means that the firearms are unloaded, separate from the driver, and located in a locked container. Despite this intended protection, some state officials will still arrest law-abiding travelers who have properly packaged their firearms, and force the traveler to invoke the FOPA as an affirmative defense in court. In other words, if your airline is diverted to New York City while traveling with your firearm, and you take possession of your baggage containing a properly packaged handgun, you will likely be arrested, cited, or detained when re-boarding your flight, unless you have a properly issued handgun permit from the State of New York. You will then have to hire a New York attorney to defend you, and assert whatever defenses may apply.

As for the transaction records that are supposed to be protected by the FOPA, there are still multiple ways the government maintains records of gun owners. Dealers must submit paperwork to governmental agencies when someone purchases multiple handguns, and that paperwork includes information about the specific firearms sold, as well as the transferee's name and address. In addition, the government maintains a database of individuals who purchase large quantities of firearms and of dealers with improper record keeping. The federal government maintains over four million detailed records from firearms tracing, which includes the personal information of the first retail purchaser and the identity of the seller.[79]

Ever wonder what happens to an FFL holder's business records (including all sales) when that FFL goes out of business? Those records must be turned over to the ATF. The ATF then enters all the records into their trace system. The information includes the purchaser's name and address; the make, model, serial number and caliber of the firearms sold; as well as all the information included on each 4473 form. Form 4473 is the detailed form completed every time you buy a gun from a dealer. In March of 2010, the ATF reported that it has received several hundred million out-of-business records since 1968.[80]

In November 1993, Congress again amended the Gun Control Act of 1968 by passage of the Brady Handgun Violence Prevention Act. The Brady Act created the national background check system (NICS) operated by the FBI. The purported purpose of the check is to prevent firearms sales to prohibited persons. The government is supposed to destroy all background check records within 24 hours.

27

Don't Be That Guy: A Few Examples of How Gun Owners Accidentally Violate the GCA

The anti-gun community postulates that it would be impossible to commit an "accidental felony." As you can now see, it is not difficult to unknowingly violate the GCA. Here are some common, but criminal, mistakes you should avoid:

Can I give this gun to my brother?

Most people feel they know their family members well enough to know whether or not they are on the GCA's "prohibited persons" list. However, while your family member may not be a prohibited person, he or she may live in a different state. The GCA does not allow you to transfer a firearm to someone who lives in a different state without going through an FFL who conducts the NICS background check. While there are limited exceptions for short-term loans or for transfers by bequest and inheritance, there is no general, familial exception to this rule.

Transfers from you to another person, when neither you nor the other person is an FFL, is called a private party transfer (PPT). PPTs are legal in many states without an FFL only when both the transferor and the transferee live in the same state. Some state laws can also affect your ability to transfer to someone in your home state. When a firearm is going across state lines, federal law requires that you use an FFL to transfer the gun to the person receiving it. There is no curing this offense. ATF indicates that those who violate this law cannot rectify their mistake. Once you have broken the law, you cannot send the gun back. Sending the gun back would actually break the law a second time. The illegal conduct has already occurred, so all you can do is hope no one cares enough to prosecute you.

Can I buy a gun for my friend?

If you are not the actual "buyer," meaning you are buying the gun for another person that is not a gift, you cannot buy a gun for another person from an FFL. Depending on your state's laws, your friend may be able to come to your state and buy a long gun from a dealer, but you cannot buy the gun and hand it to your friend. A recent court decision, *Abramski v. United States*,[81] discusses this issue, and this case is analyzed in detail in the next chapter. In short, Mr. Abramski, a retired police officer, bought a gun for his uncle, so they could take advantage of Mr. Abramski's law enforcement discount. Mr. Abramski was subsequently prosecuted and convicted of two violations of the GCA.

My husband was convicted of a felony 40 years ago, but I own the guns, so it is alright for us to have them in our home, right?

Remember that ownership is not possession. If you live with a prohibited person, that person cannot be in "constructive possession" of any firearms. If you choose to own firearms and keep them in a safe, you need to make sure the person with whom you live does not know the combination to that safe. You are also taking the risk that if you are ever charged with violating the GCA, a jury will believe that the prohibited person did not know the combination to the safe.

I regularly buy and resell guns, but it's just a hobby, so I don't need an FFL, right?

There is no doubt that many people take advantage of online firearms sales. Auction sites are like never-ending gun shows, and there are great deals and unique buys to be found. Estates are often liquidated, people are tight on money and need to liquidate a collection, or sometimes people have to sell because they are moving to a state where their firearms are illegal. Whatever the reason, online firearms sales are all the rage, and there are many buyers who take advantage of these great deals, then resell their purchases to make money.

Beware that buying and reselling firearms may require that the reseller have a license. Remember the gray and fuzzy definition of what it means to be "engaged in the business"? Be careful about how often you buy and sell firearms. If you are doing so to make a profit on a regular basis, you likely need a license.

28

When You May Buy a Gun for Another Person: Understanding the Straw Purchase Doctrine

As we have seen, gun owners, dealers, and manufacturers are all hard-pressed to learn about and keep up with the ever-evolving world of gun laws. Interpretations of the laws by various courts and agencies make it even tougher for law-abiding citizens who want to do the right thing to figure out what "the right thing" is. The "straw purchase doctrine" is a judge-made "rule" that has been additionally reduced to interpretation by the ATF, and recently, analyzed by the United States Supreme Court. This "rule" affects every gun purchaser and dealer every time a firearm is bought and sold.

Contrary to what we would like to believe, common sense does not always prevail. You might think that it would be ok for one legal gun owner to buy a gun for another legal gun owner from a licensed dealer. Neither person is a criminal, right? So what's the harm?

Well, according to the ATF, and now the Supreme Court, if you buy the gun as a gift, your purchase is legal. However, if you have been given or know you will be given money to make the purchase for the other person, you have (or will have) committed a federal offense punishable by up to 10 years in federal prison.

The reason for this result is that you have made a "straw purchase." You may have heard about straw purchases and the National Shooting Sports Foundation's "Don't Lie for the Other Guy" campaign.[82]

Taking the straw purchase doctrine to the extreme, the United States Supreme Court in *Abramski v. United States*,[83] recently turned a retired law enforcement officer into a criminal after he purchased a Glock 19 for his uncle. Both the retired officer and his uncle are law-abiding citizens who could legally possess firearms. Well, at least they were before the Court decided this case.

As most gun owners know, when someone purchases a firearm from a licensed dealer, the buyer must complete ATF Form 4473, where Question 11.a. asks:

Are you the actual transferee/buyer of the firearm(s) listed on this form? Warning: You are not the actual buyer if you are acquiring the firearm(s) on behalf of another person. If you are not the actual buyer, the dealer cannot transfer the firearm(s) to you.

Form 4473 also includes an instruction about the question, which states:

Question 11.a. Actual Transferee/Buyer: For purposes of this form, you are the actual transferee/ buyer if you are purchasing the firearm for yourself or otherwise acquiring the firearm for yourself.... You are also the actual transferee/buyer if you are legitimately purchasing the firearm as a gift for a third party. ACTUAL

TRANSFEREE/BUYER EXAMPLES: Mr. Smith asks Mr. Jones to purchase a firearm for Mr. Smith. Mr. Smith gives Mr. Jones the money for the firearm. Mr. Jones is NOT THE ACTUAL TRANSFEREE/BUYER of the firearm and must answer "NO" to question 11.a.

It is important to note that the above "instruction" is a regulation created by the ATF—it is not written in any statute and most likely, no one in Congress thought about this issue when enacting the Gun Control Act, which is silent in regards to straw purchases. What the Gun Control Act makes illegal is the transfer of a firearm to a prohibited person, such as a felon or illegal alien.

Mr. Abramski, however, answered yes to Question 11.a., even though his uncle had already paid him to buy the firearm for him. He did this because of his status as a former law enforcement officer, which allowed him a discount if he made the actual purchase.

Unfortunately, the discount was not worth what happened next: He was charged with two federal crimes for violating the provisions of the Gun Control Act. The crimes were for making a false statement "material to the lawfulness of the sale"[84] and making a false statement "with respect to information required by [the Gun Control Act] to be kept" by the dealer.[85]

Keep in mind that according to the Court and the ATF created instruction on Form 4473, if Abramski had not been paid for the purchase by his uncle, he could have legally purchased the gun for him as a gift. Under current federal law, Abramski could also have purchased the gun for himself and then resold it to his uncle at a later date. He also could have bought the gun and then raffled it off as a prize.

But, because he received money ahead of time and intended to transfer the gun to another person at the time he bought it, the court is calling the transaction a "straw purchase" and upholding his conviction for violating the Gun Control Act.

In his dissenting opinion, Justice Scalia pointed out the Court's mistake in its majority opinion:

> [T]hat false statement was not 'material to the lawful-ness of the sale' since the truth—that Abramski was buying the gun for his uncle with his uncle's money— would not have made the sale unlawful.

In other words, Justice Scalia points out that there was no illegal conduct in the transaction. There were just two law-abiding citizens in possession of a gun.

This case not only affects gun owners, but it affects how licensed dealers will conduct their business in the future. And because it is a U.S. Supreme Court ruling, it is binding on all U.S. courts.

Section III:

Where You Can & Cannot Take a Firearm, and How to Take It There Lawfully

29

THE WHO, THE WHAT & THE WHERE

Mere possession of a firearm in the wrong location, by the wrong person, or in the wrong way (loaded, open, concealed) can be a crime. Similarly, when the who, the what, and the where change because a firearm is transferred to another person, even more laws come into play to criminalize those who "do it the wrong way."

It is strange, but true, that otherwise law-abiding gun owners can be at risk of criminal charges without even drawing a gun or pulling a trigger. Some law enforcement officers may be willing to excuse an honest mistake, but

> To determine whether possession of a firearm is lawful, all of the following must be analyzed:
> 1. **Firearm**: Is the particular firearm lawful to possess under all applicable laws (federal, state, local)?
> 2. **Person**: Can the particular person in possession carry a firearm under all applicable laws?
> 3. **Location**: Is it lawful to carry in the particular location?
> 4. **Carrying ability**: Is it lawful to carry open, concealed, or loaded?

some may show no mercy. Gun owners make too many innocent mistakes by simply failing to take the time to understand the law before they possess, carry, or transfer a firearm.

In this section, we review how to be sure the possession of a particular firearm, by a particular person, in a particular loca-

tion, is lawful. We also discuss how to carry a firearm or transport a firearm lawfully and how to legally transfer a firearm to
another person. Finally, we take a look at how a gun trust can
ease some possession and transfer issues.

As you can see from the analysis in the following diagram, whether "possession" of a firearm is legal can be a complicated question. It may be legal to carry a long gun openly
on your body outside city limits, but illegal to carry a handgun
concealed within city limits without a special permit from the
government. A 17 year old may be lawfully able to carry certain
types of firearms only if certain conditions are met. What may
be legal in one place one year may be illegal the next year. The
government charges you, the gun owner, with the responsibility of keeping up with the ever-changing laws in any jurisdiction where you may possess a firearm.[86]

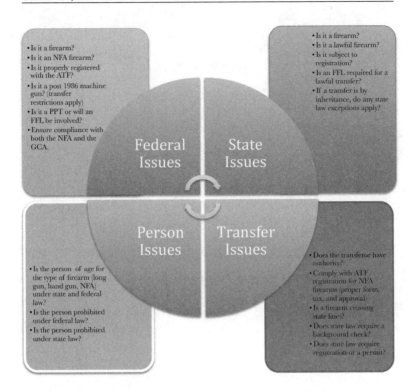

- Is it a firearm?
- Is it an NFA firearm?
- Is it properly registered with the ATF?
- Is it a post 1986 machine gun? (transfer restrictions apply)
- Is it a PPT or will an FFL be involved?
- Ensure compliance with both the NFA and the GCA.

- Is it a firearm?
- Is it a lawful firearm?
- Is it subject to registration?
- Is an FFL required for a lawful transfer?
- If a transfer is by inheritance, do any state law exceptions apply?

Federal Issues

State Issues

Person Issues

Transfer Issues

- Is the person of age for the type of firearm (long gun, hand gun, NFA) under state and federal law?
- Is the person prohibited under federal law?
- Is the person prohibited under state law?

- Does the transferor have authority?
- Comply with ATF registration for NFA firearms (proper form, tax, and approval)
- Is a firearm crossing state lines?
- Does state law require a background check?
- Does state law require registration or a permit?

157

30

IS THE FIREARM LEGAL TO POSSESS: WHAT HAPPENED TO THE FEDERAL "ASSAULT WEAPONS" BAN?

Congress passed the original "assault weapons" ban in 1994 as part of the Violent Crime Control and Law Enforcement Act of 1994. This federal law imposed a 10-year ban on 19 types of military-style "assault weapons" including many semi-automatic rifles and pistols such as AK-47s and Uzis. These rifles were categorized as "assault weapons" if they had certain cosmetic features such as folding stocks, pistol grips, and flash suppressors.

Just as with much of the state legislation banning particular types of firearms, definitions in this federal law were vague and often meaningless, and available statistics do not support the effectiveness of the law. In fact, research shows the exact opposite effect: the longer the ban was in effect, the greater the increase in murder and robbery.[87] Despite the facts, in the wake of any mass shooting, the legality of high-capacity ammunition magazines and "assault weapons" is again called into question. Fortunately, subsequent efforts to reinstate a federal firearms ban have fallen short, meaning more lawfully armed citizens can act to protect themselves and others from the criminals.

Clients have asked me to define "assault weapon." In light of the repeated and careless use of the phrase in the media

159

and particularly, on the internet, I am not surprised at their confusion.

"Assault weapon" is primarily a label invented by the anti-gun media to stir the emotions of the uninformed. I rarely come across the phrase in statutes or case law. "Assault weapon" is not defined in the National Firearms Act or the Gun Control Act. The laws of the states where I practice are devoid of the phrase, and in fact, only a handful of states in our country define or use it.

I have only become familiar with "assault weapon" because on a now daily basis it is tossed about by people attempting to gain ground on the political battlefield. It is used to promote a ban on firearms by inciting fear in the minds of people wholly unfamiliar with the design, function, and capability of various firearms. These same people repeat the phrase because of their perceived definition: "assault" must mean the firearm is more deadly than other, "normal" firearms; they must be the cause of unnecessary and senseless deaths, such as the deaths of schoolchildren.

The AR-15 is consistently targeted as a horrifying assault weapon, in part because of the misunderstanding of the "AR" designation by gun owners and non-gun owners alike. These folks use the designation as an acronym for "assault rifle" rather than understanding the true history of the AR rifles and their development by Armalite (hint: AR as in ARmalite).

What began as a U.S. military definition of "assault rifle," defined by the U.S. Department of Defense as a fully automatic rifle used for military purposes, has morphed into political propaganda. Automatic rifles fire differently than semi-automatic rifles, as one pull of the trigger will fire multiple rounds. Regardless of the misnomer, the anti-gun campaign finally succeeded in codifying an "assault weapons" ban on a national level when Bill Clinton signed the federal Assault Weapons Ban of 1994 (known as AWB and no longer in force due to its expiration on September 13, 2004).[88] The AWB itemizes specific firearms as assault weapons, as well as including those firearms that possess the "scary" cosmetic features, including detachable magazines, pistol grips, and telescoping stocks. These features were seemingly deemed by the proponents of the law to somehow make a firearm more dangerous than other firearms. However, most of the defining characteristics do not affect a firearm's effectiveness or accuracy.

The first state ban and definition of "assault weapons" was passed in California in 1989: the Roberti-Roos Assault Weapons Control Act of 1989, which together with California Penal Code Sections 30510 and 30515 itemize California's designated assault weapons. The California Attorney General subsequently published a pictorial "Assault Weapons Identification Guide."[89] California's list, if reviewed by knowledgeable firearms experts, would in most opinions include firearms that are neither military rifles nor more deadly than firearms not deemed to be "assault weapons."

All firearms can kill as intended or accidentally, as can a host of other objects willingly used by human beings for sport, recreation, or to accomplish common acts of daily living (tobacco, alcohol, and automobiles still top the list as implements of death). Tossing around a phrase to incite emotion and rob law-abiding citizens of a constitutional right does nothing to address our real societal problems.

While the definition of "assault weapon" remains elusive, use of the phrase does not.

The following rifles were banned by the former Assault Weapons Ban:[90]

(30) The term "semiautomatic assault weapon" means–

(A) any of the firearms, or copies or duplicates of the firearms in any caliber, known as–

> (i) Norinco, Mitchell, and Poly Technologies Avtomat Kalashnikovs (all models);
>
> (ii) Action Arms Israeli Military Industries UZI and Galil;
>
> (iii) Beretta Ar70 (SC-70);
>
> (iv) Colt AR-15;
>
> (v) Fabrique National FN/FAL, FN/LAR, and FNC;
>
> (vi) SWD M-10, M-11, M-11/9, and M-12;
>
> (vii) Steyr AUG;
>
> (viii) INTRATEC TEC-9, TEC-DC9 and TEC-22; and
>
> (ix) revolving cylinder shotguns, such as (or similar to)

The dreaded "AK" rifle. Photos by Oleg Volk.   *A "high capacity" magazine.*

the Street Sweeper and Striker 12;

(B) a semiautomatic rifle that has an ability to accept a detachable magazine and has at least 2 of–

(i) a folding or telescoping stock;

(ii) a pistol grip that protrudes conspicuously beneath the action of the weapon;

(iii) a bayonet mount;

(iv) a flash suppressor or threaded barrel designed to accommodate a flash suppressor; and

(v) a grenade launcher;

(C) a semiautomatic pistol that has an ability to accept a detachable magazine and has at least 2 of–

(i) an ammunition magazine that attaches to the pistol outside of the pistol grip;

(ii) a threaded barrel capable of accepting a barrel extender, flash suppressor, forward handgrip, or silencer;

(iii) a shroud that is attached to, or partially or completely encircles, the barrel and that permits the shooter to hold the firearm with the nontrigger hand without being burned;

(iv) a manufactured weight of 50 ounces or more when the pistol is unloaded; and

(v) a semiautomatic version of an automatic firearm; and

(D) a semiautomatic shotgun that has at least 2 of–

(i) a folding or telescoping stock;

(ii) a pistol grip that protrudes conspicuously beneath the action of the weapon;

163

(iii) a fixed magazine capacity in excess of 5 rounds; and

(iv) an ability to accept a detachable magazine.

Firearms previously defined as "assault weapons" by the above law, but which now circulate freely amongst the populace, still bear the mark "For Military and Law Enforcement Use Only." These firearms are often now legal to own by civilians since the ban ended, depending on applicable state law. The above list of prohibited firearms is similar to what we have now seen passed into law in several states. The next chapter addresses a few of these state laws.

31

STATE GUN BANS: THAT GUN IS SCARIER THAN THIS ONE, SO YOU CANNOT HAVE IT HERE

The last five years have proven to provide citizens with some of the strongest state gun control laws in America's history. Bans on specific rifles or rifles furnished with cosmetic parts that look scary to the anti-gun community lack supporting evidence as crime control devices, as well as any logical reasoning. Because these laws make no sense to gun owners, they are easily and often violated. In other words, gun owners fail to stop and think that taking their lawful AR-15 with a folding stock and flash suppressor from their home state into another state would be criminal . . . but it can be.

When I lived on the Oregon Coast just above the California border, I purchased my Springfield Match M1A at the local Fred Meyer. The rifle was stickered, stamped, and tagged with all manner of warnings that it was not legal to take it into the state of California, which was only minutes away. A gun purchaser may or may not get that kind of warning when buying a firearm from a dealer. If you buy a gun from a private party, it almost certainly will not come with any warning. It is your duty to know the laws of each state into which you may take your firearm.

The unsuspecting gun owner may not only be surprised by a state's law banning particular firearms, but by a state's laws that also ban certain firearms accessories. A common example is the magazine that holds more than a certain number of bullets. Again, when I lived on the Oregon Coast, it was common for residents to travel to a larger city in Oregon to go shopping. The fastest route to reach the city was often to travel a highway that wound through northern California and connected to a freeway in Oregon. One unsuspecting gun owner traveled this route to purchase some firearms-related products in the larger Oregon city. Unfortunately, he was pulled over for speeding in California on his way home to Oregon. The California Highway Patrol officer noticed that on the passenger seat in his truck was what California law deemed a "large capacity magazine," which was legal in Oregon where this man lived, but illegal in California. He was arrested for violating California's gun laws, despite the fact that he had the receipt showing he had just purchased the magazine a few hours ago in Oregon.

Why are there more state gun bans now than ever? On December 14, 2012, twenty children and six adults were killed at Sandy Hook Elementary School in Newtown, Connecticut. It was the deadliest primary or secondary school shooting, the second-deadliest mass shooting by a single person, and the second-deadliest mass shooting in U.S. history. As usual, public outcry for more gun control resulted in state legislatures passing stricter gun control laws and imposing additional burdens on citizens who wish to defend themselves from such criminals.

To help put you on alert and get you thinking about what might be illegal in a state to which you are traveling or moving, below are three of the state gun control laws passed after the Sandy Hook school shooting that ban certain firearms, magazines, and ammunition:

Colorado

Colorado's new anti-gun law caused Magpul Industries to move to a new manufacturing location. This gun ban went into effect on July 1, 2013. Magpul's decision to move from Colorado pulled an estimated $80 million from the Colorado economy and took over 200 jobs to a new location. Some of the law's lowlights are that it:

- Implemented a "universal background check" system that is required of all private transfers, with very limited exceptions.
- Made it unlawful for anyone in the state to possess, sell or transfer a "large capacity magazine." The definition of a "large capacity magazine" includes those magazines or any devices that are fixed, or detach-

Fostech Origin 12 semi-auto shotgun with a "high capacity" magazine. Photo by Oleg Volk.

able and can hold more than 15 rounds or be readily converted to hold more than fifteen rounds. The law has an exception for a .22 caliber rimfire rifle that can hold more than 15 rounds in a fixed tubular magazine, indicating that such a rifle is not included as a "large capacity magazine."[91]

- Created a crime for possessing a shotgun if it could accept more than eight shotgun shells, or hold more than twenty-eight inches of shotgun shells in an extension device.

Connecticut

On April 4, 2013, Connecticut Governor Daniel Malloy signed the inappropriately named "Act Concerning Gun Violence Prevention and Children's Safety."[92] Connecticut's new law requires gun owners to turn in or register certain firearms. Visions of the Gestapo ensued, as images appeared on the internet showing the long line of gun owners waiting to register their firearms with the government.

The public was also encouraged to report known gun owners to law enforcement. Gun owners challenged the law in court, but the Second Circuit Court of Appeals upheld the law. The Court noted that the Act "burdens" gun owner's Second Amendment rights, but the new law is constitutional because it is substantially related to the important governmental interest of public safety and crime control.[93] This outrageous Connecticut law implemented the following new rules:

- No person shall possess any "assault weapon" (with a few, limited exceptions); the "assault weapon" list identifies more than 100 semiautomatic rifles and pistols by name;

- Requires that assault weapons be sold or transferred only to a licensed gun dealer or any individual who arranged in advance to relinquish it to a police department or the department of public safety, or by bequest or intestate succession;

- Any person who moves into the state who is in lawful possession of an assault weapon shall, within 90 days, render it permanently inoperable, sell it to a licensed gun dealer, or remove it from the state;

- Bans those under 21 from purchasing semi-automatic centerfire rifles;

- Criminalizes the transfer of any firearm that is not conducted through a federally licensed dealer and subject to federal paperwork;

- Makes it a Class D Felony to possess a large capacity magazine, which is a detachable magazine that can hold more than 10 rounds unless it was purchased prior to April 4, 2013, or inherited;

- Bans the sale and transfer of all magazines with a capacity greater than 10 rounds;

New York

New York, home of the anti-gun plutocrat Michael Bloomberg, was the first state to jump on the opportunity to harness public emotion and pass strict gun laws after the Sandy Hook school shooting. The Secure Ammunition and Firearms Enforcement (SAFE) Act[94] passed in the state Senate 43-18 on

January 15, and cleared the New York State Assembly after about five hours of debate on January 16. It was signed by Governor Andrew Cuomo one hour later. The law expands the state's definition of banned "assault weapons," requires a handgun permit for all handguns, and restricts magazine capacities. This law has also been challenged in court, and one of its ridiculous restrictions was brought to light when a federal judge ruled that the Act's ban on limiting a magazine's loaded capacity to 7 rounds (with no exception for law enforcement officers) was unconstitutional.[95] Due to the law's licensing requirement for handgun owners, gun owners should not take possession of firearms from an airline, even if you are only temporarily (and unexpectedly) diverted from your travel route. Getting back on a plane to continue one's travel has posed a large problem for travelers. These unsuspecting travelers have found themselves the subject of a criminal investigation even though their handguns are properly packaged for boarding a commercial airline. One of the SAFE Act's primary lowlights is that the law makes it unlawful for any person to carry, possess or transport a handgun in or through the state unless he or she has a valid New York license.

Note that federal law provides a defense against state or local laws that would prohibit the passage of persons with firearms in interstate travel. This protection comes from the Firearm Owner's Protection Act discussed in prior chapters. Even though the FOPA provides protection to traveling gun owners, the firearms or ammunition must remain inaccessible to the gun owner. Plan your trip carefully and do not take possession of your baggage if you are diverted to New York with a handgun.

State gun laws change so rapidly that any published compendium would be quickly outdated. The internet (state legislative sites in general) is a better resource for up-to-date information about state laws, which of course, should be double-checked with a firearms attorney. One good resource is an on-line summary provided by U.S. Precision Defense, *www. concealedcarry-ccw.com*. Another good source of information is the National Rifle Association's Institute for Legislative Action (NRA-ILA).[96] The ATF also publishes a useful on-line overview of the state laws.[97]

32

POSSESSION BY PARTICULAR PEOPLE

We previously looked at the list of specific individuals prohibited from possessing a firearm under the federal law known as the Gun Control Act.

In addition to the federal list of people who cannot possess a firearm, each state may have stricter rules (a longer list of prohibited people) preventing even more people from lawfully possessing a firearm. If you are traveling with your firearm, you need to know the laws of possession in the states where you will travel if you will be making more than brief stops as you travel through the state. While you may not be a prohibited person in your home state, you may be a prohibited person in another state you are visiting.

In order to reach the right conclusion on whether a particular person is lawfully in possession of a firearm, you must address the people prohibited from possessing firearms in the federal law as well as under the applicable state's law. One of the most variable aspects of these laws between the states is the age restrictions.

33

JUVENILES, GUNS, & THE LAW

When can a child or young adult possess a firearm? It depends on the type of gun (long gun or hand gun) as well as where the young person lives (or is at the time of possession), and also on how the young person will come into possession of the gun (from a shop, from a parent, or from someone else). Both state and federal laws address when juveniles may possess or buy firearms.

The federal government is serious about keeping handguns away from minors. The federal Gun Control Act (GCA) makes it a crime for licensed dealers to sell long guns or ammu-

Photo by Oleg Volk.

nition to anyone under 18 or handguns and handgun ammunition or NFA firearms to anyone under 21.[98]

Yes, you read that right. Our service men and women may sacrifice their own lives for our country for three years (while they are between the ages of 18 to 21 years old) before they can go to a gun shop and buy a handgun to protect their own lives or the lives of their family members from an intruder in their own home. Although the NRA filed a petition to challenge this part of the Gun Control Act in 2012, the United States Court of Appeals for the Fifth Circuit ruled that the prohibition is constitutional, stating that "Congress found that they tend to be relatively immature and that denying them easy access to handguns would deter violent crime."[99]

The GCA also restricts the transfer of handguns to minors by unlicensed individuals. Friends, relatives and other unlicensed people may not sell, deliver or otherwise transfer a

Photo by Oleg Volk.

handgun or handgun ammunition to any person the transferor knows or has reasonable cause to believe is under the age of 18. In fact, federal law prohibits, with certain exceptions, the possession of a handgun or handgun ammunition by any person under the age of 18.[100] Federal law provides no minimum age for the possession of long guns or long gun ammunition.

The federal prohibition on people under 18 from possessing a handgun provides exceptions for people under 18 who possess a handgun temporarily 1) in the course of employment; 2) during ranching or farming related activities at the person's home or on the family farm or ranch land or other property where the juvenile, with the landowner's permission, is farming or ranching; 3) for target practice; 4) for hunting; or 5) while taking a course of instruction in the safe and lawful use of a handgun.

A juvenile in possession of a handgun under one of the above exceptions must have a written "note," in other words, the consent of the child's parent or guardian who can lawfully possess a firearm, unless the juvenile is merely transporting an unloaded handgun in a locked container to one of the permissible activities described. The child must have the parental consent note in his or her possession at all times when in the possession of a handgun. The possession of the handgun by the juvenile must not violate any state or local laws. In other words, if your state has a stricter law that applies to juveniles, the child must comply with the stricter law unless and until such a law is deemed unconstitutional.

Federal law also provides that people under age 18 may lawfully possess handguns if they are members of the Armed

Forces of the United States or the National Guard and are armed with a handgun in the line of duty, if they inherit title ownership (but not possession), or to defend the juvenile's life or others lives against an intruder into their home.[101]

Note that for NFA firearms, the GCA restricts dealers from selling NFA firearms to people under age 21. Young adults under age 21 can still acquire NFA firearms from private parties, through a gun trust, by manufacturing one (in conjunction with submitting Form 1 to ATF and gaining prior approval to do so), and through inheritance.

In sum, state laws regarding when young people can possess firearms vary greatly across the country. Your state's law will define who falls under the definition of "minor," and the law may have strict requirements about when a minor can possess different types of firearms. The laws restricting children and long guns (shotguns and rifles) are usually a bit more relaxed than the rules restricting handguns. Your state's laws may also have restrictions on when a gun shop or private person can transfer a long gun to a minor, even though federal law allows the transaction. For example, your state law may require the written consent of the child's parent or guardian for any transfers. So if Grandpa wants to sell his rifle to little Jonny, he may need Jonny's parents' permission before proceeding.

34

DON'T EVEN THINK ABOUT GUNS, CHILDREN, BECAUSE ALL GUNS ARE BAD, M'KAY?

Government controlled public schools across the country have implemented "zero-tolerance" policies. Enforcement of these policies means the punishment of our children if they merely think about guns. Countless children have been suspended or expelled from schools for pointing fingers like guns, playing cops and robbers, bringing toy guns to school, eating food to be shaped like guns, and even for wearing pro-Second Amendment t-shirts. Instead of teaching our children that any thought about guns is wrong, we should empower them with knowledge and teach them responsibility and ethics. Such is not the

Photo by Oleg Volk.

logic of the federal government, however.

Despite the government's position, plenty of young boys and girls enjoy shooting guns for sport and hunting. Sports teams and junior camps are becoming more and more popular. The participants are normal kids who get good grades, participate in other, more traditional "kid" sport activities, and play musical instruments. When these kids are old enough to carry concealed, they will be better prepared to protect themselves and others against an attacker.

Yet, around the country, if any of these children display "thoughts" about guns at their unprotected, public schools, they risk punishment, including expulsion. In most states, if our children choose to attend college, they risk expulsion for carrying a firearm to defend themselves on campus. While some of their parents have taught and continue to teach them to be strong and responsible, our school systems are adversely working to teach them to fear and rely upon others.

When I first read about schools expelling kids for such frivolous acts as using fingers as "guns" while playing "cops and robbers," wearing pro-Second Amendment T-shirts, or using partially eaten pastries as toy weapons, I could not believe the stories were true. Make no mistake, our government is indoctrinating our children through "zero tolerance weapons policies" to believe that weapons are bad. Unless, of course, the weapon is in the hand of a government official.

And if you're looking for the reason kids are expelled from school for having a pastry in the shape of a gun, pointing finger guns, or wearing pro-Second Amendment clothing, you need look no further than the GFSZA. When the Gun Free

School Zones Act (the GFSZA) was re-enacted as part of the "No Child Left Behind Act" (NCLBA), the revised law requires states receiving federal funds under the Elementary and Secondary Education Act of 1965 (as amended by the NCLBA) to have laws requiring local educational agencies to adopt a policy that expels students (unless modified on a case by case basis) for a minimum period of one year for bringing a firearm to school or possessing a firearm at school.[102]

Some states have responded to unreasonable "zero-tolerance" policies by passing state legislation making it unlawful for schools to enforce the policies. For example, in 2014, Florida enacted a law commonly referred to as the "Pop Tart Gun Law," in reference to the Maryland incident of teachers going apoplectic after a student ate his pop tart into the shape of a gun.

The Florida law prohibits federally funded school officials from punishing students who think about guns. The law specifically states that

> Simulating a firearm or weapon while playing or wearing clothing or accessories that depict a firearm or weapon or expressing an opinion regarding a right guaranteed by the Second Amendment to the United States Constitution is not grounds for disciplinary action or referral to the criminal justice or juvenile justice system . . . Simulating a firearm or weapon while playing includes, but is not limited to:
>
> 1. Brandishing a partially consumed pastry or other food item to simulate a firearm or weapon;

2. Possessing a toy firearm or weapon that is 2 inches or less in overall length;

3. Possessing a toy firearm or weapon made of plastic snap-together building blocks;

4. Using a finger or hand to simulate a firearm or weapon;

5. Vocalizing an imaginary firearm or weapon;

6. Drawing a picture, or possessing an image, of a firearm or weapon;

7. Using a pencil, pen, or other writing or drawing utensil to simulate a firearm or weapon.[103]

A similar bill was proposed by Representative Stockman in July 2013 in the 113th Congress. The bill was titled the "Student Protection Act." The bill states as a congressional finding that so-called 'zero-tolerance' weapons policies in federally funded schools are being used to teach children to be afraid of inanimate objects that are shaped like guns and cites examples of such punishment being inflicted upon children around the country.[104]

Like the Florida law, Rep. Stockman's bill would have prevented federally funded educational institutions from punishing students as a result of brandishing a pastry shaped as a gun, possessing small toy guns, using fingers or hands to simulate a gun, wearing a T-shirt that supports Second Amendment rights, drawing pictures of guns or possessing images of a gun, or using a writing utensil to simulate a firearm. Unfortunately, the bill did not become law. It had no co-sponsors, and according to govtrack.us, the bill was doomed from the beginning, as it had a mere 3% chance of getting past committee and a 1% chance of being enacted.

As mentioned above, the government's attempts at indoctrination extend beyond elementary and secondary schools. Adults are treated like children in most states if they tread upon a college campus, where guns are usually prohibited. A few states have passed "campus carry" laws to allow some firearms on campus. Those states with campus carry laws still have problems, because these laws can be riddled with exceptions. For example, schools can set policies that prohibit firearms in the most popular campus locations. These current prohibitions against carrying on campuses affect more than the students. They affect all university patrons, such as those attending football games and other events. The exceptions to the ability to carry on campus may also prevent students from bringing firearms to the dormitories. When one considers these huge holes, it is apparent that these laws suffer from a "feel good" compromise syndrome. Where is the protection for young women if they cannot carry a firearm to events and to the place where they sleep? While some guns are certainly better than no guns, even in the states allowing some ability to carry on campuses, the exceptions allow the criminals an advantage.[105]

We cannot continue to have a "take what we can get" attitude. While the legislative process can be tedious, corrupt, and controlled by organizations other than "we the people," "we the people" still cast the votes. We cannot remain satisfied with mediocre, compromised legislation or the politicians who support it. We cannot continue to sit back and watch what is happening on the news without taking action. Some of our politicians have what it takes to stand up for what is right, and others do not. You are responsible for educating yourself and finding out who will be your voice. Will you elect a constitutional conservative or a sell-out? You will make a difference if you educate yourself, educate others, and vote. Join zero tolerance, pro-Second Amendment organizations such as Gun Owners of America as well as your state's grassroots organizations. Educate yourself, and speak up. You can effect change by getting involved and by supporting the organizations working on behalf of gun owners.

35

WHAT HAPPENS IF THE WRONG PERSON GETS YOUR GUN?

Very simply, you can be sued. Worse, you could be charged with a crime.

Being a responsible gun owner means you safely secure your firearm wherever you may be and regardless of whomever may be around you. Your firearm should only be accessible to you and to people to whom you purposefully make it available.

Some states, like California, allow parents to be charged with a crime if the parent fails to secure firearms from children under the age of eighteen.[106] Punishment for violation of the California law varies, depending on whether the child actually uses the firearm to inflict injury. Adults can be imprisoned for up to three years and fined up to $10,000 for violating this law. Even in states without specific laws making it criminal to allow children access to guns, prosecutors can still charge parents or other adults with crimes such as "reckless endangerment" for leaving a firearm accessible to others.

For example, a man was prosecuted in Oregon for recklessly endangering other people, after an evening at the movies with his wife. He attended the movie with his gun holstered. Unfortunately, the weapon was not securely holstered. After returning home, he discovered it was no longer holstered. He called the theater to ask someone to look for it, but no one answered. He returned to the theater the next morning to discover that the theater was holding a special showing for high school students. One of the students discovered the gun on the floor near his seat. While this story had a happy ending because no one was hurt (the student turned the gun in to the theater staff), it could have taken many different turns with terrible outcomes.

The handgun in the Oregon case was fully loaded with a round in the chamber. The district attorney decided to prosecute the gun owner for recklessly endangering others.

The moral of this story is simple: If it is your gun, it is your responsibility. Do not be irresponsible or lazy when it comes to your firearm. Imagine how much worse the above situation could have been if the special theater showing the next morning was for grade school children instead of high school students, and the trigger was pulled.

Even if you are not charged with a crime against the public, a private person can still sue you in civil court if you allow another person, who should not have a firearm, to access your firearm, and the person injures an innocent person with it. This type of lawsuit is known as a case of "negligent entrustment."

The legal theory of negligent entrustment allows other people to sue you when you allow another person to use a "thing" or to engage in an activity that is under your control, and you know, or should know, that the other person intends or is likely to use the "thing" to create an unreasonable risk of harm to others. The most common example of negligent entrustment is when someone hands their car keys to a drunk. The law says that if you hand keys to an obviously drunk person, you made a mistake. Because you could have prevented the injury caused by your mistake, the people who were harmed by your mistake may sue you.

The law treats allowing a minor access to a firearm similar to allowing a drunk access to a vehicle. This area of negligent entrustment law is expanding, meaning that individual people continue to file new court cases where they claim to be the victims of other people's mistakes. Think about this: If the act of entrusting a loaded firearm to a minor satisfies the criteria for negligent entrustment, then the entrustment of a loaded firearm to others who may "notoriously misuse" the firearm may also allow for a cause of action for negligent entrustment. Those who "notoriously misuse" a firearm would likely include people with a propensity for violence, such as convicted felons and the mentally ill.

To be sued for negligent entrustment, you do not have to physically hand your gun to the other person. If you simply leave your firearm in a place where a child, felon, or someone else you know may be likely to misuse it would come across it, such as in an unlocked dresser drawer in an unlocked bedroom, you can be sued.

Never forget that your firearm is your responsibility. If other people are harmed by your negligence, you harm the entire gun owning community when the tragedy is publicized.

36

LANDOWNERS TRUMP THE SECOND AMENDMENT

Many gun owners, particularly employees of private businesses, feel their right to carry is violated when a private land or business owner does not allow guns on their property. Your right to self-defense by using a firearm is taken away when you choose to enter a store or to accept employment with a business that restricts firearms on its property.

This situation is created because, with very limited exceptions, our laws respect the freedom of property owners to set their own rules; if you do not like the rule, do not go onto the other person's property. This is a hard pill to swallow for people who want to shop at retail establishments that forbid firearms, and for Americans who love their jobs but cannot bring a gun to work.

While it seems unfair to make someone choose whether to exercise their right to self-defense or have a job, most laws currently side with the property owner. Some states have carved out exceptions to this general rule to protect employees, and this effort is discussed in more detail later on.

37

GOVERNMENT PROPERTY: LEAVE YOUR RIGHT TO SELF-DEFENSE AT THE DOORSTEP, PLEASE

Even when you are lawfully in possession of your firearm in your home or in public, your right to self-defense does not necessarily extend beyond certain doors. Many government and private buildings are "gun free zones."

Federal Buildings

Federal law prevents you, with limited exceptions, from bringing a firearm inside a "federal facility."[107] A "federal facility" is a building, or part of a building, owned or leased by the federal government, where federal employees are regularly present for the purpose of performing their official duties. The exceptions to this general rule are for the usual, uniformed public protectors: officers, agents, and state or U.S. employees performing their official law enforcement duties and federal officials and military members, if authorized by law to possess a firearm. The unusual exception written in this law is for people carrying firearms for hunting or other lawful purposes. Despite this exception, I doubt that any federal government personnel will allow me to walk into a federal facility with my handgun, which I am carrying for self-defense (a lawful purpose) or walk through a federal building with my hunting rifle. Not surprisingly, this is another legal gray area, and it remains unclear as to which activities the exception applies.[108] Whatever it may contemplate, the exception does not apply to a federal court.

Also unclear to the average gun owner is what sort of "facility" will constitute a prohibited place. A change in the federal laws in 2010 made it lawful for gun owners to carry a firearm in a federal park. Just because you tour Yellowstone (or any other federal park) with your sidearm ready, do not think you can lawfully see all the sites with your self-defense mechanism. For example, caves located on federal land constitute federal facilities for purposes of this law, so be sure to check your gun with your coat at any cave entries. Also, state law can restrict your carrying ability on federal land, so again, make sure you comply with both the federal and state laws.

Violators of the federal law will be faced with maximum sentences, depending on the violation, ranging from one to five years.

Federal Forests, Federal Parks, and other Federal Land

Federal law does not prevent you from taking your firearm onto National Park land and within National Wildlife Refuge Systems, but your state law may have restrictions on whether you can carry your firearm loaded, concealed or open on such land. Discharging a firearm in a National Wildlife Refuge is prohibited.[109]

A National Forest is a different type of land regulated by the Department of Agriculture. It is illegal to discharge a firearm in a national forest within 150 yards of a residence, building, campsite, developed recreation site or occupied area, across a road or body of water adjacent to the road, or in any manner or place where a person or property is exposed to injury or damage as a result of such discharge or into or within any cave.[110]

Bureau of Land Management (BLM) land is mostly regulated by the state's law where the land is located; however, federal law prohibits discharging firearms on developed recreation sites and areas unless specifically authorized.[111]

Note that the government claims it is "here to help." If you have questions about the laws pertaining to a particular area of land, ask at the government office managing the land. The same applies for land managed by state or local governments—ask the rules before you carry or discharge your firearm on government property.

State Government Buildings

The federal government does not control whether you can carry a firearm inside state government buildings. State laws may restrict firearms in certain buildings. The usual restricted buildings include courthouses, jails, and juvenile detention centers.

Laws forbidding firearms inside state buildings vary between the states. Some states allow lower governmental entities, like counties and cities, to impose stricter laws on possessing firearms inside buildings. Most prohibited buildings proudly post that guns are not allowed inside the building, but relying on whether or not a sign is up is not foolproof. If you are not certain, get legal advice before proceeding.

38

THE DEADLY FAILURE OF GUN FREE ZONES

Pro-Second Amendment Americans are not in any way enlightened by the repeated tragedies at our military bases and our schools. Rather, we sit back and watch a horrific version of the decades-old movie "Groundhog Day," with a consistent replay of criminals killing helpless victims in gun free zones.

In these gun-free zones, Americans are disarmed every day when they go to school or to work. The laws "protecting" military bases and schools, as well as employers' policies, strip citizens of their right to self-defense.

These failed attempts at gun control must be recognized and stopped. Since the inception of gun free zones, several bills have surfaced to repeal the laws, but all have failed. The research and the statistics that criminals select these kill zones have been proven over the last three decades. Americans must prove that we are not a country that will knowingly leave our young children and the adults willing to protect and defend them vulnerable to terrorists and psychologically disturbed killers.

Twenty-five years have passed since Congress enacted the Gun Free School Zones Act (GFSZA) in 1990. Similarly, Department of Defense (DoD) Directive 5210.56 was signed into effect in February 1992 by Donald J. Atwood, Deputy Secretary of Defense under President George H.W. Bush.

Prior to the GFSZA, it was legal for American kids to drive the family pickup to school with a gun rack and rifle in place. But after the Stockton, California schoolyard shooting, Congress passed this "feel good" law, creating a new venue for killers to make their fame. The GFSZA made it a federal offense "for any individual knowingly to possess a firearm at a place that the individual knows, or has reasonable cause to believe, is a school zone."[112] Unless a person meets the requirements of the law's few exceptions,[113] an American carrying a firearm within 1000 feet (close to three city blocks) of a public, parochial, or private school will face a $5,000 fine and up to 5 years in prison, and the loss of their right to possess a firearm for life.[114]

Surprisingly, and for the first time in over half a century, the United States Supreme Court ruled that Congress exceeded its constitutional authority to regulate interstate commerce by passing the GFSZA.[115] Congress, however, quickly revised the law. The new version of the GFSZA prohibits possession of "a firearm that has moved in or that otherwise affects interstate or foreign commerce" in "a place that the individual knows, or has reasonable cause to believe, is a school zone."[116] This new law remains unchallenged and is currently in effect.

At least nine of the country's ten deadliest school shootings have followed. At least ten school shootings killing at least four people have occurred since the bill's original passage, compared to only two such killings for the 20 years prior to the law. These shootings, and the increase in deadliness of them, are shown in the chart on the next page.

In fact, with only two exceptions since 1950, all of the mass public shootings have occurred in gun-free zones.[117] Research

The Most Deadly School Shootings Have Occurred Since the GFSZA Was Passed

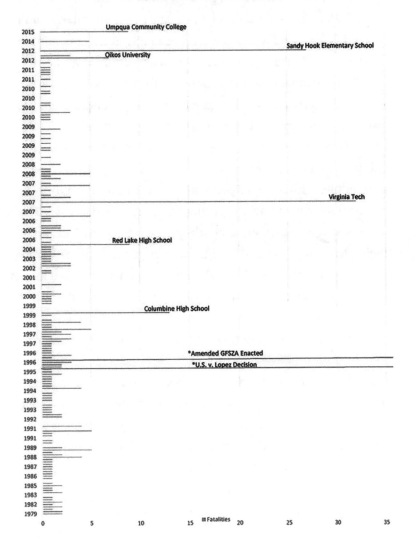

197

definitively shows that the states with the fewest gun free zones have the fewest gun-related killings, injuries, and attacks. On top of that, the killers boldly proclaim in their diaries and through social media how they intentionally avoid committing their crimes in locations where gun owners could stop them.[118]

To those who still subscribe to the theory of common sense, a "gun free zone" is an obvious "killing zone," where the criminal is in control. The primary failing of all gun free zone laws is that these laws remove firearms from the sheep (our children or non-carrying adults) *and* the sheepdogs (responsible adults who are charged with protecting our children or responsible gun owners carrying for personal defense). The logic is simple: Without sheepdogs nearby, the wolves kill at their pleasure. Time and again, these killers do not randomly start shooting in public. Instead, they intentionally select a location where they have control—gun free zones offer them this opportunity.

There is a growing movement in state legislatures across the country to fight against Congress and take action to eliminate the GFSZA and other "gun free" zones, such as military bases and private places of employment. Some states have already passed legislation specifically allowing teachers to carry firearms to protect their students or prohibiting employers from enacting gun free workplace policies.

Recently, the tiny Idaho town of Garden Valley made national news when its board went a step further. This bold Idaho school board voted to go beyond giving its teachers permission to arm themselves. The Garden Valley School District expended taxpayer dollars to purchase firearms for its schools and to post signs to inform criminals that the school is armed. Similarly, the town of Greenleaf, Idaho, officially asked its residents to acquire firearms and receive training on how to use them for self-defense. In a beautiful twist to the "gun free zone" signs that abound across our country, the town of Greenleaf proudly posts signs that it is NOT a gun free zone.

Unfortunately, ignorant parents would deny their own children the protection the Garden Valley school board has offered. Parents were quoted by the media as commenting that the plan was "ridiculous" and that the school should "work on security guards" instead of arming the faculty. The liberal media, of course, did not like the idea of guns in the hands of responsible adults either. These anti-gun people went so far as to comment that children might be afraid to "speak out" against a teacher, knowing the teacher was armed. Wouldn't children in fact feel safer knowing that their teacher is also their protector, with firepower ready to defend the class? Perhaps . . . if our federal and state governments would stop indoctrinating our children to believe guns are evil.

Nothing illustrates the madness of mythical "gun-free zones" like the media's pictures of the Chattanooga military base crime scene: a gun-free decal with bullet holes nearby.

Americans must take a stance and support these efforts rather than simply express disgust at the law.[119] Change occurs in the face of adversity. Supporting organizations and the efforts of our senators and representatives who are willing to take a stance and destroy the killing zones is the duty of every American. Join your local organizations and national organizations to fight these unconstitutional laws.

Photo by Oleg Volk.

39

GUNS AT THE WORKPLACE

Every day, millions of Americans are disarmed as they go to work. Some work locations, such as military bases and schools, are governed by "public safety" laws and policies, which allow only members of elite statuses, such as security guards, on-duty law enforcement, or politicians, to carry a firearm. Other locations are governed by the policies of private business owners who may be afraid of the liability of allowing their employees to carry guns to work and instead, implement their own, fear-based "gun free" work place policies.

My law firm not only supports employees carrying guns to work, we reward employees by paying the cost for them to take defensive firearms training. I implemented this policy because I have been personally subjected to these gun free zone laws and policies when I was an employee. Most courthouses do not allow firearms except in the hands of on-duty law enforcement officers. Most prosecutors have offices in the county courthouse. While I served as a prosecutor, I made enemies of the sociopaths I took off the street. Most sociopaths make their way back to the street, usually sooner than they should. During this time, I was supposed to depend on others to protect me, even when leaving work alone at night and walking to my car. I vowed to never put my own employees in the same position.

Federal law does not regulate guns at private workplaces. Even though nearly two million Americans report being the victims of workplace violence each year,[120] our Supreme Court has not yet provided us with specific guidance on whether disarming Americans while they work, and on their way to work, is unconstitutional. The Occupational Safety and Health Administration (OSHA) has published works available to employers in a supposed effort to guide them on a path to prevent workplace violence.[121] These publications are full of "tips" for employers to address violence against social workers, late-night retailers, taxi-drivers, and other high-risk groups of employees. If these publications were not so sad, they would be comical in their complete absence of any suggestion that employees carry a firearm for self-protection. Fortunately, there is a movement by state governments to protect Americans' Second Amendment rights while they work.

The movement to protect employees began in Oklahoma, and laws now exist in at least 15 states across the country, protecting employees in various ways. These state laws sprung up initially to prevent the egregious policies of some business owners, which prevented employees from storing firearms locked in a vehicle parked in a company parking lot. These "parking lot" policies not only disarm workers while at work, they disarm them on their travel to and from work. Unfortunately, such policies are still lawful in most states across the country, but again, thanks to gun owners who are willing to make an effort and pro-Second Amendment organizations, the wheels are in motion to eliminate them.

The state laws that have been enacted differ in what and how they protect employees, but the following are some of the issues the laws address:

- Protect employees' rights to store firearms in their private vehicles even when parked in the employer's parking lot.
- Limit an employer's ability to search vehicles on its property.
- Prohibit discrimination against gun owners.
- Subject an employer to fines for failure to comply with the law's restrictions or requirements.
- Provide protection to employers that comply with pro-Second Amendment laws, including immunity from injuries arising out of compliance.
- Specify that employers can allow weapons at the workplace without violating the OSHA general duty to provide a safe work environment clause.

What are employers afraid of? Being sued is a big concern. If guns are not banned, and the employer hires the wrong person, a victim of gun violence might sue the employer for not preventing the violence. This type of a claim would be hard for a victim to prove against an employer, and on top of it, simply having a policy that bans guns at the workplace without a mechanism for enforcing the policy does little to protect an employer. A violent employee will carry out his or her intentions with or without a firearm. Hiring procedures that include a psychological exam and a thorough background check on prospective employees are much better preventative measures. Yet, most employers (even those who do not allow firearms) fail to implement these two simple mechanisms to prevent work-place violence.

Advice for Employers

Our firm regularly prepares employee handbooks that include policies against violence that are protective of employers while allowing employees to carry their firearms to work. If you are an employer and would like to implement such a policy, here are a few tips:

1. Screen your employees before you hire them, and always, always, conduct a thorough background check. A safe workplace begins with the hiring process.

2. Set requirements for training—if your state laws allow you to do so. At a minimum, require that your employees have a state concealed carry permit, which means they have passed a background check conducted by law enforcement.

3. Establish requirements for storage and control of the firearm. Leaving a firearm unattended inside the workplace where it is accessible to others is grounds for termination without discussion.

4. Ensure that employees have read your firearms policy and have had an opportunity to ask questions.

5. If not prohibited by your state's law, implement a reporting system for employees who carry. Employees should at least annually update you with proof of their training. They should also at least annually sign a declaration stating they are not a prohibited person under state or federal law.

6. Have a self-reporting policy that requires employees to report immediately to their supervisor if they become a person who is prohibited from possessing a firearm.

7. Make sure you have a procedure for other employees to report threats of violence.

40

PLANES, TRAINS, AND MOTOR BOATS . . . TRAVELING WITH YOUR FIREARM

Commercial Airplanes

It can be legal to bring a firearm into an airport—depending on how you are carrying the firearm. State law dictates whether the firearm can be loaded or whether it must be packaged a certain way at all times once you step onto airport property.

Federal law prevents you from carrying a firearm and ammunition into a "sterile" area of the airport. I experience too many calls from people who have unknowingly left a loaded magazine, single bullet, or some other item considered a weapon in a range bag doubling as a travel carry-on, only to have it discovered while going through the TSA checkpoint. There is rarely any leniency for the gun owner in this situation. And if the item you forgot in the bag turns out to be a concealed "dangerous weapon" that would be accessible to you while on, or trying to get on, a plane, you can be imprisoned for up to 10 years for your forgetfulness.[122] If you are not arrested at the airport, then upon your return home, you can expect a letter from the TSA informing you of your violation. The typical letter outlines your options to pay, submit evidence in your defense, or request a conference or hearing. I strongly urge gun

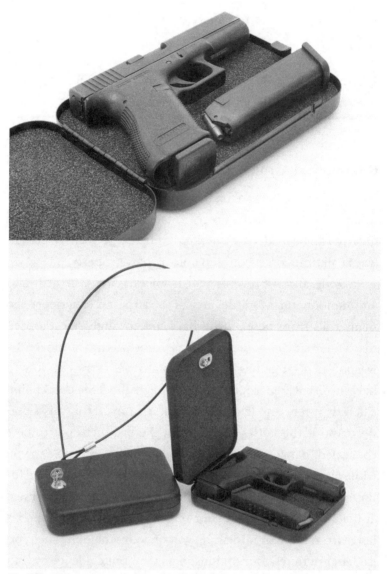

Typical airline-approved gun safes. Photos by Oleg Volk.

owners to use a separate bag for air travel, one that you never use as a range bag, to eliminate the possibility of leaving a firearm, magazine, or ammunition in your travel bag.

As usual, certain elite groups are excepted from the gun-free airport laws: the restrictions do not apply to law enforcement officers authorized to carry arms in their official capacity and anyone authorized to carry by the Federal Aviation Administration (FAA) or the Secretary of Transportation.[123] There is also an exception for people who are transporting "unloaded" firearms in baggage that will not be accessible to them during the flight, as long as the air carrier is told about the firearm. The FAA approves gun safes that can be locked and stowed in checked bags, so long as the traveler declares to the airline agent any firearms that may be in the bag.

Commercial and Private Pilots

Federal law imposes restrictions on both commercial airlines and private pilots.

Commercial airline pilots may not carry a firearm unless they volunteer to participate in the Federal Flight Deck Officer program. These flight crew members, which includes pilots, engineers, navigators, and other flight crew personnel, are deputized federal law enforcement officers authorized by the Transportation Security Administration to use firearms to defend against acts of criminal violence or air piracy undertaken to gain control of their aircraft. The FFD officers undergo training on the use of firearms and the use of force. The program requires that the participants remain anonymous and only share their participation on a need-to-know basis.

State law can provide some relief and exceptions for private pilots, depending on whether the pilot is flying a common carrier.[124] State statutes may allow a private pilot and the pilot's invited guests to have firearms on a private plane if the firearms are properly stored or in the custody of the aircraft's pilot. State laws also may allow hunters chartering an aircraft for hunting purposes to take their firearms aboard the aircraft or place the firearm in the custody of the pilot of the aircraft. The trickier questions remain for pilots who may find their way to a "sterile area" of the airport—those areas come under federal law and those federal laws must be observed in addition to state laws.

Passenger Trains, Buses, and Other Public Transportation

Federal law requires that when you cross state lines with a common carrier, even if the carrier allows firearm possession, you must declare and surrender the firearm to the carrier operator for the trip.[125] Each individual company may also implement their own policy regarding whether or not you can carry a firearm while using their transportation service.[126]

Boats and Waterways

Whether you can carry a firearm on a boat depends on where your boat is in the water. International, federal, state, local or even another country's laws may apply. The United Nations Convention on the Law of the Sea (UNCLOS) provides some guidance.[127] Generally, boating within three miles of a state's shoreline subjects you to both state and federal firearms laws. Boating within twelve nautical miles of the shoreline is

U.S. territory (territorial waters), where only federal firearm laws apply. Between 12 miles and another 12 miles is known as the "contiguous zone," and from there to 200 miles you are in what is called the "exclusive economic zone (EEZ)." From the EEZ to 350 miles you are in the "continental shelf." If you proceed beyond the continental shelf, you are either in international waters or another country's waters. You should at a minimum check with the ATF and Customs and Border Protection to ensure you have any necessary permits or fulfill any other requirements to enter another country's waters or to re-enter U.S. waters with firearms. Because these rules are not only complicated, but in some circumstances unsettled, you should consult with a maritime attorney before engaging in your boating activities with a firearm.

41

CONCEALED, OPEN, LOCKED & LOADED, OR INACCESSIBLE & EMPTY?

If your firearm is lawful, you are lawful, and your location is lawful, the analysis is still not yet complete as to whether you are lawfully in possession of your firearm. You also have to make sure that "how" you are in possession, in other words, how you are "carrying" the firearm, is also legal.

Concealed carry laws can very quickly make criminals out of otherwise law-abiding citizens. I recall a particular case in Oregon, where the prosecuting attorney attempted to make a criminal out of an upstanding physician. This citizen was an experienced, generous doctor who traveled to a rural community to devote time to patients in that area of the state who needed his services but had trouble traveling very far on their own. This doctor had no criminal background whatsoever. He did, however, have an Oregon concealed carry permit.

In the midst of his busy life, this doctor did not realize that his concealed carry permit had expired (by less than a month). He was pulled over for a minor traffic violation, and honestly answered the officer's question that he had a gun with him in his vehicle. He then told the officer he had a concealed carry permit, and handed it to the officer with his driver's license. The officer noticed the permit was expired, and cited the doctor for the crime of unlawful possession of a firearm. The prosecuting attorney filed the charge, and refused to reduce this crime to a lesser charge. Instead, the prosecuting attorney (who was not in favor of guns) insisted that the doctor plead guilty to a crime and face up to one year in jail and a $5,000 fine. This case is a reminder that those who have the authority to prosecute you do not always apply common sense to a situation.

"Carry" laws are primarily governed by the state law where you wish to carry the firearm. On occasion, a federal law may dictate how you may lawfully carry a firearm, such as when checking a firearm in luggage at an airport. Local ordinances can also restrict your carrying ability. For example, some counties or municipalities do not allow firearms to be carried loaded in a public place, or they place licensing restrictions on carrying a loaded firearm.

State law similarly controls whether you can carry your firearm "open" or "concealed," and whether your firearm can be carried "loaded" or whether it must be "disassembled" or even "locked" and "inaccessible" to you. Most state laws prohibit carrying a firearm concealed without a license. Some states distinguish between handguns and long guns, and allow long guns to be carried concealed without a license. These concealed carry laws are also often riddled with exceptions for people engaged in certain activities, such as hunting or shooting at a range. Concealed carry laws do not, however, provide any exception for someone who simply wants to carry for the reason the Second Amendment protects our God-given right to carry: self-defense.

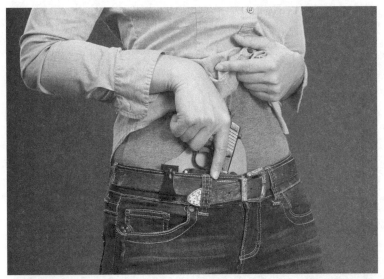

Concealed carry.

Open carry. Photos by Oleg Volk.

The "open versus concealed carry" philosophical debate continues within the gun-owning community. Concealed carriers have decided to bite the government bullet, give up their private information and money, take a basic training course (no matter how experienced the gun owner) and obtain a special license. All of this effort is accomplished so the gun owner may legally tuck a firearm under an article of clothing, carry in public, or (in some extreme locations) simply possess a handgun. Gun owners who carry their firearms openly run the risk of harassment or even arrest for brandishing their firearm if a member of the public reports being threatened by the presence of a firearm.

Some state laws allow open or concealed carry without requiring any special permit for law abiding gun owners. Other states take the exact opposite approach by banning the practice of open carry and requiring a permit for concealed carry.

These various carry laws bring up a number of questions, all of which must be answered by the applicable state and local laws. What is a concealed firearm? What is a loaded firearm? What is a public place?

When is a firearm concealed?

If you think you are open carrying in a place that allows the practice of open carry, but you are actually carrying a firearm that is deemed concealed under the law, you might be arrested and convicted of a crime. The behavior that will constitute the concealed carry of a firearm is a product of each state's law. Each state has its own definition by statute and case law interpreting the meaning of the word "concealed."

At its simplest definition, "concealed" means that the firearm is not immediately visible to someone else, such as when a handgun is tucked inside your waistband in front and not visible from behind, or when your handgun is tucked into your car's door or between the seats and not visible from your driver's side window to an approaching law enforcement officer.

Simply because a firearm is visible from some possible angle does not mean that it is not concealed. This is the part of the law that seems to cause many gun owners problems. For instance, a firearm that is visible from the passenger side window of your car, but not visible from the driver's side window, will usually be considered concealed. The less the gun is visible, the more likely it is that a court will find that it is concealed.

The determination of a concealed firearm can become even more complicated in states with strict gun control laws. For example, in California, "concealed" can include a magazine that is ejected and near the firearm but that is not visible, even though the firearm is openly visible.[128] The court in the California example decided that a loaded magazine tucked under an ashtray made the firearm that was in plain view on the passenger seat of the car available for use and a threat to public order. If you are unsure, you should assume that concealing any part of a firearm may be a violation of the law.

Some law enforcement officials treat innocent misconduct for what it is, take the opportunity to educate the gun owner, and move on. My own policy as District Attorney was to allow law-abiding citizens charged with unlawfully carrying a concealed weapon (and nothing else) to obtain their concealed carry license and avoid prosecution. I preferred to save our tax dollars for the real criminals. But not all prosecutors are reasonable—especially not the anti-gun ones. Any technical violation of the law will be used by those opposing the Second Amendment as a means to have someone's gun forfeited and the gun owner's rights taken away.

Your best defense to being charged with a crime related to the concealed carry of a firearm is to have a valid concealed carry permit from a state whose permit is accepted in many other states. Note that even though you have a license to carry concealed, such a license does not override other laws that prohibit taking firearms into certain locations such as sterile areas of an airport or into government buildings where firearms are prohibited.

Those with concealed carry permits must also be mindful of leaving a concealed firearm in a vehicle driven by others. This problem frequently stems from the misunderstanding of what it means to own and to possess. Some family members fall into the trap of believing that if they leave "their" handgun in their car, and they have a concealed carry permit, it does not matter if a spouse or other family member drives the car. It actually matters a lot. If you leave a concealed firearm in your vehicle, whoever drives the car may be breaking the law if the driver does not have the necessary concealed carry permit.

If you are not going to get a concealed carry permit, it is best to prominently display your firearm to avoid an arrest and potential conviction in a state where open carry is allowed, or to unload your firearm and secure it (and secure any ammunition separately) in the trunk of your vehicle, where it is not accessible to you while driving.

What is a loaded firearm?

What constitutes a loaded firearm is defined by the respective state law you will be applying. "Loaded" means different things depending on the law you are applying and the type of firearm. Generally, "loaded" means there is ammunition in the firearm—whether there is a round in the chamber or merely rounds in the magazine or somehow attached to the firearm. If you have both the firearm and ammunition together, you should realize that you may have a loaded firearm under the law, and must not carry it in public without meeting the legal requirements for doing so. Note also that some laws require not only that your firearm be unloaded, but also that it be inaccessible.

What is a public place?

Some states have laws restricting the carrying of a loaded firearm in a public place. These laws, of course, beg the question of what constitutes a "public place." A public place can either be referring to a government maintained location, such as a park or government building, or may be referring to any location open to the public, whether the place is owned by the government or by a private person, such as a restaurant, mall, the street, a sidewalk, or parking lot. A good rule of thumb is if the "place" is a location where you, the "public," can access it without special permission, then the location may be a "public place" where carry restrictions, such as a prohibition on carrying a loaded firearm, may apply.

If the complicated analysis of how you may carry a firearm outside your home frustrates you, you are not alone. Congress

217

has had multiple opportunities to simplify these carry laws and require concealed carry permits from a gun owner's home state to be recognized by all states. Press your politicians to get such legislation passed.

In the meantime, check laws at *concealedcarry-ccw.com* and at *nraila.org* before carrying a firearm outside your home state. You should confirm and review your findings with your firearms law attorney.

42

DISPELLING CONSTITUTIONAL CARRY MYTHS

Concealed carry laws are governed by each individual state. The result is that the laws can vary widely between states, and travelers must be wary and knowledgeable of the laws in the jurisdiction to which they are traveling. This, of course, poses a hardship for law-abiding gun owners who do not wish to be prosecuted for committing a crime simply because they were confused about the law in a certain location.

Over the last decade, legislation has repeatedly been proposed to afford concealed carry permits the same recognition as driver's licenses in each state, but such proposed legislation has routinely failed to pass in Congress.

Another option to address the complexity created by 50 states with 50 different versions of carry laws would be to pass legislation allowing law-abiding gun owners not only to *own* a gun, but to *carry* their firearm without obtaining additional governmental permission. This type of law is referred to as "constitutional carry."

Constitutional carry reflects the view that the Second Amendment to the United States Constitution permits no restrictions or other regulations on gun ownership for law-abiding citizens. In other words, if a person is not prohibited from *possessing* a gun, they should be allowed to *carry* the gun where and how (open or concealed) they wish to carry it without first obtaining additional, special governmental permission. After all, the United States Supreme Court has held that our right to keep and bear arms is protected for self-defense purposes. It does no good to own a gun for self-defense if you cannot take it with you to defend yourself.

Constitutional carry legislation allowing gun owners to carry firearms openly or concealed and without an applicable permit or license is a growing trend. Multiple states already allow law abiding gun owners to carry their firearms without special licensing. More states are proposing legislation that would allow constitutional carry.

Currently, however, most states continue to require concealed carry permits. As bills for constitutional carry are proposed around the country, it has become apparent how misguided the public, including some politicians, are about what constitutional carry actually means.

The politicians who ignore the truth and who fail to comprehend the correct concept of constitutional carry flagrantly mislead the public. I have heard politicians openly proclaim that they cannot support constitutional carry because such a law would allow criminals to possess firearms. Such a position is patently wrong. Constitutional carry will not override the federal Gun Control Act. All the "bad people" who are prohibited from possessing a gun still cannot carry a gun legally. I have also heard politicians argue that constitutional carry will allow known gang members to carry firearms and inhibit law enforcement's ability to arrest these gang members.

Coming from a law enforcement background, I am all about getting the bad guys off the street. However, if all you have for evidence is someone carrying a gun, you do not get to play judge and jury and call that person a criminal. If the person is on probation or has been convicted of a felony, is a drug user, is engaging in criminal behavior, or falls into a host of other "prohibited person" categories, then we already have ample laws that prohibit that person from possessing firearms. The concern that constitutional carry would expand the ability of criminals to possess guns is therefore misplaced.

On a more optimistic note, state legislatures are continuing to propose constitutional carry so that law abiding gun owners do not have to maneuver through government bureaucracy to exercise their right to carry for self-defense purposes. Again, this is only happening because people like you and me are getting informed and getting involved.

43

How to Know If Giving a Gun to Another Person Will Break the Law

Transferring a firearm includes much more than selling a firearm. The legal definition of "transfer" often includes selling, assigning, pledging, leasing, loaning, giving away, or *otherwise disposing of* a firearm.

To analyze whether any transfer of a firearm is lawful, you must consider a number of different factors:

1. Type of transfer (PPT or FFL?)
2. Type of firearm (NFA or regulated by state law?)
3. Transferee (the person receiving the firearm must be legal in all respects)
4. Transferor (the person transferring the firearm must have authority to do so)

Type of Transfer

How a firearm is being transferred is the initial question in any transfer situation. The "type of transfer" inquiry focuses first on whether the transfer is between a federal firearms licensee (FFL) or between two unlicensed people (called a "private party transfer" or "PPT"). A PPT takes place when one gun owner transfers a firearm to another gun owner, and neither person is an FFL. The transfer rules are different for PPTs.

223

Many federal and state laws, rules, and regulations apply to FFLs that do not apply to private parties. Many of the rules on how an FFL can transfer a firearm are found in the Gun Control Act. Some of the laws are also found in the National Firearms Act. State laws can also apply to FFLs, so it is important to address the state laws where the firearm is originating as well as where it is going. No matter where the FFL conducts business, the FFL must conduct a NICS background check or apply one of the few exceptions to doing the check and ensure that the transferee (the person receiving the firearm) completes ATF Form 4473 before transferring the firearm. FFLs can transfer all firearms across state lines to another FFL.

While the rules are different, the Gun Control Act also restricts transfers between unlicensed individuals. You cannot transfer a gun to someone whom you know, or reasonably should know, cannot possess a firearm. With very limited exceptions, you cannot transfer a firearm to a person who lives in another state unless you involve an FFL to complete the transfer to the transferee, regardless of how well you know the other person or even when the other person is a family member. In fact, one of the most common violations of the GCA's transfer rules is for unlicensed individuals to transfer a firearm across state lines without involving an FFL.

Federal law (the GCA) requires PPTs between residents of different states to take place through an FFL in the recipient's home state. While it is possible to ship long guns through the U.S. Postal Service and handguns through UPS or FedEx if certain restrictions are met,[129] many FFLs do not accept firearms shipped to them by anyone other than another FFL. Your sale to another person who lives in a different state from you may therefore involve an FFL in your state taking possession of the firearm, sending the firearm to an FFL in the state where the buyer lives, the buyer completing an ATF Form 4473 and a NICS background check at that FFL's shop, and the buyer then receiving the firearm.

I have received calls at my office from private people selling guns across state lines, to double check what they were told by gun store personnel, who have misinformed their customers. This truth is a reminder that you should not ask non-lawyers for advice on the law. The risk and consequences are too great to get bad advice.

If you are transferring a firearm to a person who lives in the same state you do, federal law does not require that you use an FFL. Be careful, however, to make sure that you follow your state's laws regarding private party transfers. Some states require "universal background checks," meaning that you must use an FFL even though you are transferring a firearm to someone in your home state. Even if your state does not require a background check, using an FFL or at least requesting a copy of the recipient's concealed carry permit can protect you from being accused of knowingly transferring a firearm to a prohibited person. The FFL can ensure that the recipient is not a prohibited person and also of the proper age.

There are a few exceptions to the general rule of using an FFL for PPTs between people who live in different states. For example, the GCA allows transfers to people who live in other states without using an FFL if your transfer to them is a temporary loan or rental of the firearm for lawful sporting purposes.

In other words, if a friend who lives in another state would like to borrow your hunting rifle to go hunting in his home state, you may loan it to him (temporarily) without using an FFL, so long as neither state has laws that would restrict this process. The GCA also allows the transfer of firearms across state lines without involving an FFL when someone inherits a firearm.[130] Again, state law may restrict this process.

Federal law also recognizes that a person can maintain a home in more than one state, and makes an allowance for this situation. If you are a resident of more than one state, you can legally purchase firearms in each state during the time that you reside there. In other words, when you are at your home in Sun Valley, Idaho, you can buy guns at the nearest Idaho gun shop. When you return to your home in Scottsdale, Arizona, you can buy firearms from your local dealer there. Be sure to understand what "resident" means for each state where you maintain a home. Often, having a vacation home is not enough to establish residency in a state.

Type of Firearm

Any analysis of whether a firearm transfer is lawful must consider the firearm involved. Is it a conventional (non-NFA) firearm? Is it regulated by state or federal law or both? Again, be sure to consider the state laws in all involved states—the laws of the state the firearm is leaving as well as the laws of the state where the firearm is going must be considered.

If the firearm is an NFA firearm, paperwork must be completed for most transfers.

The most common type of NFA transfer occurs on ATF Form 5320.4, known as "Form 4." This form is used whenever someone purchases a new NFA firearm from a dealer or when an NFA firearm is transferred from person to person, unless a "tax free" exception applies. When using Form 4, the appropriate tax (usually $200) must accompany the form when it is sent to the ATF. When the transfer is to an individual (as opposed to a gun trust or business entity), the individual must also complete a certificate of residency, get the approval of the chief law enforcement officer where the individual resides, and submit a photograph and set of fingerprints. Whenever you buy a suppressor, machine gun, or a short-barreled rifle or shotgun, you will need to wait for the ATF to approve the transfer and put a "stamp" on your Form 4 before you can receive your firearm.

A common exception to the taxable transfer using Form 4 is the tax free transfer of estate firearms. This type of transfer can occur using ATF "Form 5," and no tax need be submitted with Form 5. There are, however, pitfalls with this exception. One of the common ones is whether the transfer is mandatory. In other words, if the decedent's will states that an NFA firearm must be distributed to a named person, or if the decedent did not leave a will and the NFA firearms will be distributed according to state law to the person's natural heirs, then the transfer will be "tax free." If the NFA firearms will be sold as part of the estate or distributed to a gun trust that is not required or otherwise distributed to people who are not required (by a will or the law) to receive the firearms, the distribution will be taxed and the transfer must be approved using Form 4. Either way, the paperwork must be approved by the ATF before the transferee takes possession of the firearm.

ATF Form 5320.20 aka "Form 20" is used when you travel with your NFA firearms from one state to another, temporarily or permanently. This form must be submitted to the ATF Branch at least 45 days before the firearm will leave one state. Form 20 is not required for every firearm. Suppressors are a notable exception to the requirement of completing Form 20, although the ATF urges you to complete its Form 20 for suppressors as well as for the required firearms.

The Transferee & The Transferor

Making sure that the transferor has the authority to transfer the firearm (is the lawful owner or is the lawful administrator of an estate, trust, or business entity) is essential to legally transferring a firearm. If the person does not have the authority to transfer, either someone else will need to make the transfer or a court order may be needed to allow the transfer.

Similarly, the transferee must meet all the requirements under both state and federal law to receive the firearm—be the right age for the type of firearm, live in a state where the firearm is allowed to be possessed, and not otherwise be prohibited from possessing the firearm.

44

INHERITING GRANDPA'S GUNS: THE FAMILY HEIRLOOMS THAT "GO BANG"

As with any other transfer issue, firearms in estates or trusts must be analyzed by addressing the transfer in light of all applicable state and federal laws.

When a gun owner dies, the first question should always be whether the firearms are secure. If the registered owner has died, did that person leave a firearm (possibly loaded) where others (possibly non-gun people) have access to it? The firearms should be stored in a way where only the person who will administer the estate or trust (assuming that person is not a prohibited person) will have possession of them, and also a place that will make theft unlikely.

If a person in charge of an estate or trust does not secure the firearms, that person can be sued for negligent entrustment or even charged with a crime.

Once the firearms are secured, the second inquiry must be who can be in lawful possession of the firearms. When a person dies, the court usually appoints a personal representative (also called an executor or executrix) to take control of all the estate assets. The personal representative will consequently be in "constructive possession" of the firearms, and the personal representative can legally transfer the firearms to other people or sell them. If a gun owner dies after transferring of all his or her firearms to a gun trust, other people should be designated as successor trustees in the trust, and those successor trustees can lawfully possess the firearms without any action by a court. If the personal representative or the successor trustee is a prohibited person (cannot legally possess firearms), then another person must be designated to possess and transfer the firearms to the intended recipients.

The third inquiry is to determine what types of firearms the person owned, and whether any of them were illegally owned. If you are in charge of an estate as a personal representative or a trustee for the person who died, you must determine whether the estate includes any NFA firearms and if so, to whom they are registered. If you are unable to locate any paperwork showing the registered owner, then the personal representative of an estate can request this information from the ATF in writing. When you make this written request to the ATF, you will have to disclose your identity and the identity of the firearm in question. If the estate owns unregistered NFA firearms, the unregistered NFA firearms cannot be possessed or transferred. The personal representative for the estate should immediately contact the ATF and arrange for disposal of any unregistered NFA firearms, as it is not legal for the personal representative to remain in possession of them. If the firearm was illegal for the original owner to possess, then it is illegal for anyone else to possess. The person delivering contraband to the ATF is shielded from prosecution. If you have additional questions, it would be a good idea to contact a firearms attorney.

If the NFA firearms *are* properly registered, remember

that there is still paperwork to be completed and approved prior to transferring the firearms. It is not uncommon for an unsuspecting spouse to possess NFA firearms unknowingly. You should also make sure that any transfers you will make comply with the laws of any of the states in which the firearms will wind up.

If the estate assets include firearms that are not NFA firearms, then all of the laws and rules we have discussed about possession and transfer must be addressed. The person in charge of the estate or trust must determine whether any heirs are prohibited from possessing firearms. If so, then such a prohibited person cannot receive their inheritance. Before transferring any firearms in an estate, you must check ages and the laws of the states where the heirs live. Different states have different age requirements for firearms, and those age requirements sometimes depend on the type of firearm. Some firearms are prohibited in certain states, and obviously, you cannot transfer firearms to a state where they are not allowed.

The best practice, before transferring firearms in an estate, would be to use the services of an FFL or at least require a copy of the heir's concealed carry permit. Remember that some states may require that an FFL be used to conduct a background check before any transfer can take place, and some states require registration of certain firearms.

Some important questions that have to be answered when firearms are transferred in an estate include:

- Are the lawful heirs allowed to be in possession?

- Are any of the firearms subject to the National Firearms Act, which would require the filing of paperwork for approval by the ATF?

- Are any of the heirs underage under federal law or in the states where they live?

- Are the guns going across state lines?

- Are the guns legal in the states where they are going?

These are just a few of the questions that have to be addressed when guns are to be transferred in an estate.

45

THE TRUTH ABOUT GUN TRUSTS

When properly written, gun trusts are powerful asset protection and estate planning tools. A well-drafted gun trust will achieve the following for the gun owner who creates the trust:

1) Ensure that friends and family can lawfully possess and transfer trust owned firearms during the gun owner's lifetime;

2) Create a private plan that completely avoids the court system for all firearms if the gun owner becomes incapacitated or dies;

3) Eliminates most of the bureaucracy involved when acquiring NFA firearms;

4) Helps the successors and heirs to understand the gun owner's desires related to all the trust-owned firearms;

5) Helps the ones you care about to comply with firearms laws when they possess or transfer the firearms;

6) Assists the gun owner to own firearms in more than one state; and

7) Ensures that neither the gun owner nor any loved ones commits an accidental felony.

Despite all of the above benefits, gun trusts have become popular mostly for another reason: The trust will allow the creator of the trust to lawfully share NFA firearms with people named by the creator in the trust as trustees. Recall that without a gun trust, only the registered owner of an NFA firearm may possess that NFA firearm.

As with many gun-related topics, misinformation is spread by the unknowing to the unknowing with respect to what a trust can and cannot accomplish. A gun trust is much more than a piece of paper that proclaims to create a gun trust. Gun trusts are legal entities ("persons" under the National Firearms Act) with many of the same rights as individual people. If you are going to rely on a document that purports to create a "gun trust" to actually be a "gun trust," your best bet is to consult with a qualified attorney to make sure you know what your "supposed" trust actually does.

> **A gun trust is much more than a piece of paper that proclaims to create a gun trust.**

Because so many people ask my opinion on various "form" trusts, I will expand on the problems with cheap, non-lawyer drafted trusts. First, I have yet to review an internet or gun shop obtained "gun trust" form with a client, where the client actually understands the limitations of the form. At best, an NFA trust form will qualify as a valid trust and "person" in the state where it is signed by the creator of the trust. At worst, the trust is not a valid trust, does not therefore create a "person," and any creator or trustee of the trust is in unlawful possession of NFA firearms supposedly owned by the trust.

One of the most common mistakes made by gun owners who purchase a ready made NFA trust (usually online or at a gun shop) is believing they have purchased a trust that will "hold" and protect their firearms for their children and descendants. In fact, these trusts are really nothing more than an NFA trust that names multiple parties who can be in possession of NFA firearms as trustees—that is, only until the creator of the trust becomes incapacitated or dies. I have yet to review a free or cheap form trust that properly provides for the trust creator's incapacity, death, or descendants. I have reviewed many form trusts and trusts created by lawyers who do not actually understand the gun laws. These trusts fail in many ways to provide and protect the gun owner's firearms and family. Even the ATF recommends that gun owners seek the advice of a firearms attorney before preparing a gun trust.

The following are a few of the common problems with "form" trusts:

- They are generic and lack firearms-specific guidance;
- They permit or even direct illegal firearms transfers;
- They permit prohibited persons to possess firearms;
- They are often invalid, incomplete, or defective;
- They lack the backing of a knowledgeable gun trust lawyer when trouble comes your way.

You should also know that there are different types of gun trusts. A gun trust can be a simple NFA trust, a revocable gun trust, or an irrevocable gun trust. The differences between these trusts are profound. The following paragraphs describe the differences for you.

1. **NFA Trust:** An NFA trust is designed to create a legal entity that will be recognized as a "person" under federal and state law. This trust is purposefully created to allow multiple people (trustees and beneficiaries) to be in lawful possession

of National Firearms Act firearms (mainly suppressors, SBRs, SBSs, and fully automatic firearms). NFA trusts rarely address the incapacity and death of the trust creator, thus leaving transfer upon these occurrences to the creator's other estate planning documents.

2. **Revocable Gun Trust:** A revocable living gun trust is intended to own all firearms. Its terms can be changed (amended) or revoked. This trust includes special instructions pertaining to laws related to the possession and transfer of all "firearms" as that term is defined under state and federal laws, as well as all firearms accessories. These items do not necessarily have to be listed anywhere in the trust. The trust should contain provisions that will prohibit unlawful transfer and possession by the trustees of the trust.

3. **Irrevocable Gun Trust:** This type of gun trust is designed to pass a legacy to future generations. The irrevocable gun trust is an asset protection and tax planning gun trust, which is designed to last much longer than a revocable gun trust. This type of trust can provide ultimate protection against the claims of creditors and predators.

46

Understanding General Trust Concepts

If you are going to understand what a gun trust is and what one can accomplish for you, you need to have a basic understanding of trusts in general.

The definition of a trust is that it is "A legal entity created by a grantor for the benefit of designated beneficiaries under the laws of the state and the valid trust instrument."[131]

There are three main players in the trust world:

1. **Grantor:** Depending on the state's laws, this person may also be called the "Settlor" or the "Trustor." In essence, the Grantor is the "creator" of the trust—the person who sets the trust up and signs the trust documents.

2. **Trustee:** Think of the Trustee as the "manager" of everything the trust owns. The Grantor will decide what property initially is transferred to the trust he or she creates, and the Trustee will then make decisions about what can be done with the trust assets. The Grantor and the Trustee may be the same person.

3. **Beneficiary:** A trust Beneficiary is the person who enjoys the benefits of the trust assets. For example, you might set up a trust for a child. You would be

237

the Grantor, and you could also be the Trustee if you name yourself as such when you create the trust. If you are both, you might put $100,000 in the trust for your child, and then as Trustee, you will decide where the money goes, what expenses to pay, and what to do with the trust income (adhering to any direction you gave in the trust). The child, however, is the Beneficiary. You are only managing the trust money for the child's benefit.

There are many different kinds of trusts lawyers create for their clients, depending on what the lawyer intends to accomplish for the client. A trust may be created for tax planning, to protect young children, to save an inheritance for a disabled child, to take care of a pet, or simply to plan for the trust creator's own death and incapacity.

The most common type of estate planning trust is called a "revocable living trust." This type of trust is a self-contained plan for the person who created it (the Grantor) with provisions for how property will be managed if the Grantor becomes incapacitated (also called disabled, depending on the state) and what will happen when the Grantor dies.

The Grantor or Grantors (joint revocable living trusts are often created by spouses) transfer their assets to the trust and serve as the trustees of the trust. The Grantor or Trustees continue to have full control of the assets held by the trust— they can buy, sell, manage and control the trust assets just as

> No one needs to rely on government systems to direct how they will be cared for if they become incapacitated or what will happen to their possessions when they die.

they would if they had not transferred them to the trust. In other words, the Grantor continues to conduct business as usual with respect to the assets he or she has transferred to the trust.

When the Grantor dies or become incapacitated, the trust names the "Successor Trustee" who can step into the Grantor's shoes to control the trust assets. A successor trustee can be anyone the Grantor has named in the trust—family, friend, bank, financial advisor, or attorney. No court approval or process is required.

The trust will state who the new beneficiaries of the trust will be when the Grantor dies (in other words, who inherits the trust assets). The trust assets can go directly to these beneficiaries or stay in trust for greater protection.

A properly created and funded revocable living trust will prevent the Grantor from needing a court-ordered guardian or conservator if the Grantor is incapacitated with respect to the trust property. The trust will also prevent the trust assets from being "probated" (having to go through the court process) when the Grantor dies. In other words, the creator of a revocable living trust com-

Lawyers who were fed up with the inefficiencies of the court system created the living trust to protect their clients and their clients' assets from the inefficient, public court probate system. When I explain the difference between having a Last Will & Testament coupled with a General Durable Power of Attorney versus a Revocable Living Trust plan to my clients, I focus on the power the client is taking back from the government: You create the rules with your trust, not the government.

pletely bypasses the court system by preparing a trust. Trust planning is a legal way of taking control of your own affairs and possessions if you die or become incapacitated. It is the best way to take care of yourself and your family without government intrusion.

Rather than being the unwilling subject of default state laws and an overburdened, complicated, and costly court system to decide what will happen to you when you are incapacitated (and to determine whether you ARE incapacitated), your trust alone dictates what "incapacity" means, who decides whether you are incapacitated, and who steps in to manage the trust property and provide assistance to you if you do become incapacitated. You can also provide detailed instructions directing your named successor trustee on what to do with the trust assets upon your incapacity. Recall our discussion of what it means to be "adjudicated a mental defective" under the Gun Control Act. Proper trust planning will avoid that problem for the gun owner, because the court should not be involved when a gun owner has created a trust plan. Instead, the gun owner's trust plan takes the place of the court system.

A gun trust is a trust with all of the above features, plus it is specifically designed to provide added protection for firearm possession and transfer. A proper gun trust will dictate who will distribute your firearms when you die or become incapacitated, and where the property will go upon either of those events. As such, the trust is a substitute for a Last Will and Testament and replaces the probate court system with your own customized, self-contained plan.

If you do become incapacitated, rather than entrusting the government with the power over deciding who will be appointed as your guardian or conservator, and how you should be cared for, and how your assets (including your firearms) will be dealt with, and hoping the government does the right thing, you dictate all of these terms when you create a trust. If you become incapacitated, you do not have to leave your personal affairs to the government to figure out through the public (meaning not only that you have access to the public court, but because it is public, everybody has access to you) and inefficient court system. The same is true upon death. Why leave a Last Will & Testament (which must be submitted to the court when you die) and allow a judge you do not know to oversee what happens to your assets, when you can create your own system via a trust instead? With a properly constructed trust plan, you have created your own plan for incapacity and death, and the people you choose can step in and follow your plan when something happens to you. That is what should happen, and that is exactly what a properly constructed gun trust should do as well.

47

Why Every Gun Owner (Especially Married Couples) Should Have a Gun Trust

A gun trust is a special type of trust that is designed to hold all of your firearms and firearms-related accessories. Gun trusts assist with the process if you become incapacitated or die, boost possession capabilities under the NFA, and expedite the acquisition of NFA firearms. Let us address the estate issues first, by way of some examples of what can go wrong upon a gun owner's incapacity or death.

Estate Example #1

In my first example, a widowed father created a generic Last Will & Testament online. He wrote in the form that he wished to leave his entire firearms collection to his beloved son. Unfortunately, by the time the father passed away, the son had been convicted of a domestic violence offense. The father never updated his Last Will and Testament, and he did not know enough to leave an alternate plan for the firearms in the online form, or even to simply state that if for some reason one of his heirs could not receive a specific gift outlined in the will, the heir would receive something else in place of the specific gift (such as stating that if his son could not receive the firearms or the firearms no longer existed at the time of his death, that the son would receive cash or some other property of similar value in place of the firearms).

The father also wrote in the form that he wished for his other child, his responsible, hard-working daughter, to act as his personal representative (also known as an executrix).

Like many children, the daughter and her brother met at their dad's home after his death to divide his personal belongings. During that process, the daughter gave all of the guns to her brother, and he drove them back to his home in California.

The daughter and her prior lawyers did not have a clue that she and her brother broke the law. Gun laws do not always require that the violator have knowledge of the criminal law violation for charges to be filed. The poorly drafted will in this situation left no alternative gift to the son, did not name an alternate beneficiary to receive the guns, and did not in any way address the laws pertaining to the possession or transfer of the firearms.

This scenario is a classic example of an "accidental felony." The daughter knew her brother was convicted of a domestic violence offense, but did not understand the laws enough to refrain from giving him guns. Her behavior is typical of many children inheriting firearms from their parents—they do not know enough to stop and think about all the rules they must obey when transferring the guns to the intended recipients.

Estate Example #2

An aging wife is concerned about her husband's declining mental capacity due to Alzheimer's. She is worried about being able to manage their affairs on her own, because his retirement plan administrator denied her access to information on her husband's separate retirement account when she called to ask a few questions. The couple never completed any estate planning documents—no will, no trust, no power of attorney, no health care directive. This woman's husband has a gun collection that includes NFA firearms. She was never interested in firearms, has no idea of their value, and would prefer to have nothing to do with any guns (except to sell them so she can have more money to care for her husband). She took a couple of the full-autos to a gun shop for an appraisal, but was asked to leave (and also frightened) because she did not know anything about any paperwork they were requesting to see. The wife just committed an "accidental felony" by unlawfully possessing and attempting to transfer the NFA firearms.

The husband, in this example, is the only person who can be in lawful possession of the NFA firearms. For the wife to have lawful possession, she will need to proceed to the court to ask the judge to appoint her as her husband's legal guardian and conservator in order to transfer the firearms to herself or others. Once a guardian or conservator is appointed, the husband will be "adjudicated a mental defective" and become a prohibited person under the Gun Control Act. At that point, the husband cannot be in possession or constructive possession of any firearms. His wife will either need to transfer all of the firearms out of the home or, at a minimum, lock them in a safe and not tell her husband the safe combination. The NFA, the GCA, and state law dictate what the wife's options are in this example.

How Gun Trusts Would Have Solved the Above Problems

Let us take a look at how a properly drafted gun trust would address the above situations.

When someone has a well-written gun trust, the people named in the trust to manage property if the creator of the trust dies or becomes incapacitated will have a wealth of information available to them in the trust document itself. My gun trusts read like books, and my clients often comment on how much they have learned about gun laws simply by reading their trusts. Because all this information is in the trust document, the successor trustee will be alerted to many issues that can create potential civil and criminal liability. We will assume for the remainder of our discussion that the gun trust that could have been created for the people in my examples was well written and that it included all the things a competent firearms attorney would include in the trust.

GUN TRUST SOLUTION FOR EXAMPLE #1

If the father had created a gun trust instead of a Last Will and Testament, these accidental felonies would have likely been avoided. The trust would have, in black and white, prohibited the transfer to the son and alerted any attorney and the personal representative to his status as a "prohibited person" because of the domestic violence conviction. The trust would have clearly outlined who "prohibited persons" are under both state and federal law. There would have been no question that the son could not have legally received the firearms. In other words, the criminal behavior would have been completely avoided.

The trust also would have made it clear that the son was not entitled to any substitute assets in lieu of the firearms, to eliminate any fighting amongst the remaining heirs. The trust would have directed that the guns go to the father's alternate beneficiary (the daughter) to sell or keep, depending on her wishes.

The firearms would also not be listed in any public court proceeding, because firearms owned by a gun trust do not need to be "probated" when the creator of the trust dies. Whoever received the firearms would have been able to receive them quickly, efficiently, and without court paperwork or a public record.

Gun Trust Solution for Example #2

When a spouse becomes incapacitated, the other spouse's primary concern is usually to care for the incapacitated spouse. The typical secondary concern is how to come up with the financial means to do so. The last thing a person in this situation wants to do is go to court, have his or her spouse ruled by the court to be mentally incompetent, and invest the time, energy, money, and stress involved in all aspects of filing a court proceeding. A well-planned gun trust could prevent this situation from occurring simply by making the wife a trustee or beneficiary of the trust.

In my second example, a gun trust would have named both the husband and his wife as trustees and as beneficiaries. Even when only one spouse is interested in the guns, most couples understand that the gun trust will prevent any issues down the road when the primary gun owner dies or becomes incapacitated. The gun trust would have been the registered owner on all ATF paperwork for the NFA firearms. Because the trust, rather than the husband, would have been the owner, the wife, as a trustee, could possess or transfer those firearms on behalf of the trust.

The need for a guardian or conservator with respect to the firearms would have been completely eliminated, and there would be no fear of violating any laws if the wife decided to take some time to keep the firearms in the home, sell them one by one to achieve top dollar, or transfer them to other people. The gun trust would have given her complete legal authority to do whatever she needed to do (or what the gun trust dictated she should do), such as give the guns to children, grandchildren, friends, or any other named beneficiaries in the trust. Again, the court system, the delays, and the fear of violating the laws would have all been eliminated with a properly planned gun trust.

Summary of Gun Trust Benefits

As you can see, gun trusts have invaluable benefits over no plan or even a will-based plan. Trust planning in general provides a more seamless plan for incapacity and death, and in the realm of firearms, it is by far superior because it deals specifically with firearms laws.

When clients create a will-based plan, they often also sign a "Durable Power of Attorney," where they name someone to act on their behalf if they are incapacitated. Any firearms law-related provisions are almost always entirely missing from these documents. A gun trust will cure issues related to named agents' or trustees' lack of knowledge about your guns and gun laws and will prevent them from committing an accidental felony. Trusts are also usually private, and they avoid guardianships, conservatorships, and after-death probate.

48

WHAT DOES A WELL-DRAFTED GUN TRUST LOOK LIKE?

There are some similar attributes found in well-written gun trusts. A gun trust should hold legal title to all NFA firearms and provide control of all firearms and firearm related accessories to the named trustees. The gun trust should allow the desired people to lawfully share the firearms and accessories during and after the trust creator's life without violating state or federal possession laws. Similarly, the gun trust will only allow legal transfers of firearms to allow the named players to buy, sell, loan, lease, or bequeath the firearms. The trust should also allow the trustees to store firearms in multiple locations – including in different states.

The gun trust will keep the court system's nose out of the gun owner's firearms collection. The gun trust should also provide meaningful guidance to the other trustees and beneficiaries (who may not be gun people) on the gun laws and how to avoid committing an accidental felony. In short, the trust should contain guidance that will help the trustees and beneficiaries acquire, possess, and transfer any and all firearms within the law.

A well-written gun trust plan will also address specific concerns about spouses, create a dynasty trust for children when desired, and even give to charity when desired. The trust can build a family armory, preserve an antique collection, and store resources for disaster preparedness. The trust can be created to protect the firearms from "creditors and predators." These provisions address specific desires for your firearms legacy and passing on that legacy to the right people.

49

How a Proper Gun Trust Cures NFA Possession & Transfer Issues

Gun trusts are designed to eliminate the court process and ensure that no laws are violated. The trust ensures the laws are followed. The trust contains specific instructions for lawful possession and transfer of all firearms and firearm related accessories. The possession and transfer issues addressed throughout this book will be addressed in a well-drafted gun trust.

A well-drafted firearms trust is also designed to address the unique laws that apply to NFA firearms. The gun trust specifically allows for any named trustee, successor trustee, and certain beneficiaries to have the ability to use the trust assets. There may even be a provision that will deem any person that you go shooting with a trustee of the trust. The gun trust will specifically ensure that the NFA is not violated with respect to NFA firearms.

Under the NFA, you may acquire NFA firearms individually or through an entity. Individual ownership is not the best way to own NFA firearms, because only the individual in whose name the weapon is registered will be entitled to use (or even possess) the items. The ATF defines the term "unauthorized transfer" broadly, and depending on the circumstances, that definition will even include allowing a spouse to have the combination of the safe where the firearms are stored.

As a result of the drawbacks of individual ownership, many gun owners eagerly create a gun trust to purchase and hold NFA firearms. Using a trust simplifies the process of acquiring NFA firearms.

Corporations, LLC's, and non-profit corporations can also be used to obtain NFA firearms. One problem with these entities is that they all require fees to be paid to the state in which they are organized. They also create a public record, because they must be registered with the secretaries of state where they are created and where they transact business. You must pay an initial fee to form the entity and in most states, a yearly fee to maintain it. Further, these types of entities are designed to earn money, not to hold, share, and distribute assets. Homeowner's and umbrella insurance policies may not cover assets owned by a business entity, requiring a separate insurance policy for the gun owner's "business."

In contrast, a legitimate trust does not ordinarily require any fees with the state and is not a matter of public record. Because trusts are primarily an estate-planning tool, they are designed to hold, share, and distribute assets.

Before choosing a gun trust attorney, clients should question their potential gun trust attorney about that attorney's prior experience with gun laws. At a minimum, they should ask the following questions:

1) Where did you learn about the gun laws?
2) Do you have any gun-related criminal law background?
3) Have you written any articles or taught gun law classes?

4) What estate or business gun-law related issues have you resolved for your former clients?

If your estate or business involves firearms, make sure your attorney is well-versed in both state and federal gun laws. After all, there are thousands of gun laws on the books, and without significant prior experience, you should question the attorney's ability to protect you. Remember, each attorney's particular knowledge and experience that they can offer to their clients is different. It is important to remember that each attorney has particular knowledge, experience, and expertise; that not all attorneys are created equal, and not all gun trusts are created equal.

50

THE FUTURE OF GUN TRUSTS

After the Newtown school shootings in 2013, there has been much discussion about a new law proposed by the ATF specifically targeting gun trusts: Rule 41P. This rule was signed on January 1, 2016 as Rule 41F.

Gun trusts are not eliminated by this rule, but one of the benefits of having a gun trust will be. The rule requires that a "responsible person" of a company or trust be photographed, fingerprinted, and send a notice to the chief law enforcement officer (CLEO). The concern, according to the federal government, is that criminals are using entities to avoid a background check, and thereafter obtaining firearms regulated by the National Firearms Act without a background check. This assertion of course, is false, because even when a trust fills out the ATF paperwork to obtain a tax stamp, a human being always has to pick up the firearm, and that human being still completes Form 4473 the same as they would for any other dealer-acquired firearm.

Although the government provides no statistical support for its conclusion, it proposes a "fix" for the phantom problem—a "fix" that will cost taxpayers an estimated $3,000,000.00 annually. The cost for the ATF to process the responsible person information is estimated at $1.8 million annually. The estimated cost to state and local agencies for processing paperwork is $1.2 million. Ask your state's teachers if they can afford to sacrifice even more of their salaries to unnecessary bureaucratic nonsense.

According to the ATF, the petition for the rule change was originally submitted to the ATF in 2009 by the National Firearms Act Trade and Collectors Association (NFATCA). The ATF claims that the NFATCA expressed concern that firearms subject to the National Firearms Act (primarily full automatics, suppressors, and short barreled rifles and short-barreled shotguns) may wind up in the hands of people who intend to commit violence. The Department of Justice, of course, agreed with this undocumented concern of the NFATCA, hence the rule change. However, the NFATCA has taken the position that while they acknowledge that their petition expressed concern regarding "prohibited persons receiving firearms without background checks via trusts and corporations, the draft NPRM does not reflect any discussions or negotiations we have had with the Federal Government regarding same."[132]

The undesirable effect on most individual gun owners of the new rule is that a "responsible person," which includes any individual possessing, directly or indirectly, the power to direct or cause the direction of the management, policies, and practices of the legal entity, insofar as they pertain to firearms must submit a photograph, fingerprints, and a CLEO notice on an application to receive or make an NFA firearm.

The ATF reviewed the 9000+ comments submitted by gun owners and businesses before the new rule was finally signed into law. I will continue to bring you updates to the implementation of Rule 41F on the Gun Law Podcast, and my Gun Law bLAWg.

SECTION IV:

THE SECOND AMENDMENT'S ULTIMATE PROTECTION— DEFENDING YOUR LIFE WITH DEADLY FORCE

51

INTRODUCTION TO DEADLY FORCE

Owning a firearm is a personal choice that carries with it specific and rare responsibilities. In deciding to own a gun for self-defense, you must be willing to take another person's life to protect your life, the lives of your loved ones, or perhaps the lives of people you don't even know. You must also commit to being safe and efficient while using the firearm, and to understanding the laws that pertain to the use and ownership of your firearm.

There are varying degrees of self-defense, all of which relate to the probability of causing severe bodily harm or death. When you use a firearm in self-defense, its use is considered "deadly force." Deadly force is the ultimate level on any use of force continuum, as it carries with it the greatest probability of inflicting severe bodily harm or death. Many gun owners lack basic legal knowledge about the use of deadly force. Even though people may keep a gun by their bed or even carry one in their car or on their person, they often cannot explain the circumstances under which they can legally shoot or even kill another human being with their firearm. With thousands of gun laws in force across the country, and very little training focused on the law, this information can be difficult to attain.

My passion and mission not only for my clients who own guns, but for every American, is to share the knowledge I have acquired as a gun owner, a student of the use of deadly force, a planning attorney, and a prosecuting attorney. I have personally led major crimes teams on homicide investigations to determine whether the shooter lawfully used deadly force or committed murder. In some of these investigations, we determined that the shooters lawfully used deadly force to defend their lives or the lives of others. I have also successfully defended clients who have used firearms in self-defense.

> Having worked self-defense cases from both sides, I wish to share my insight on what you as gun owners can do to protect yourselves and your families and still go home to be with your loved ones after a deadly force event.

Having worked these cases from both sides, I wish to share my insight on what you as gun owners can do to protect yourselves and your families and yet remain free of criminal prosecution.

In an effort to help every gun owner understand more about the responsibilities of owning a firearm, I have compiled a list of critical items everyone should know. These are things I wish I had known when I was personally attacked. Fortunately, I escaped and had a chance to learn them.

The following chapters contain basic concepts every gun owner should understand, commit to memory, and instantly apply in a self-defense situation. Keep in mind the information provided here is limited and is intended to help you understand the basics of deadly force and realize how much there is to learn. My hope is that this information inspires you to seek out more training and information so you can be optimally prepared should you ever need to use deadly force against another person.

52

Won't It Look Bad If I Train Too Much with My Firearm?

Thanks to our media and the prosecution of those who lawfully use deadly force, conscientious gun owners sometimes fear that their lawful, responsible behavior puts them at risk for being deemed a "gun nut." When it comes to training, do not let such a fear stop you.

Even though I grew up with guns and shoot whenever I can, I also train whenever I can. One of my first gun instructors served our country in combat, but told me he continues to train whenever he can. He was the first person to tell me that you can never train too much, and no matter how good you think you are, it is important to continue to train. What a lesson for all of us.

Many of my clients have sought my advice on how often to train with their firearm. They worry whether it will look bad in court if they have had significant training. The truth is, if you are a gun owner, you must be deadly accurate with your firearm. You need to shoot and kill the right person (instead of innocent bystanders) when you are under extreme stress—mind racing, heart pounding, and hands shaking. If your life is threatened, you will rely on instinct to make split-second decisions, and you cannot afford to be wrong! If you are wrong, you will either be dead or in prison. You have to know how to react in a life or death situation, and the more training you have, the more likely you are to instinctively handle the situation.

Because of my criminal law background, I know how to effectively build the prosecution's case and cross-examine a defendant on trial for using deadly force. And I can tell you, if you own a firearm, you can NEVER have too much training. While some lifestyle choices can cause an increase in legal fees because your lawyer will have some explaining to do, too much training is not a lifestyle choice that will be a concern. In fact, you had better be deadly accurate with your firearm, because it is the lack of training and knowledge (using the wrong ammo, hitting an innocent person, etc.) that will dub you as irresponsible and that will be detrimental in a criminal trial.

Do not fool yourself into thinking that because you

The author, instructing her student. Photo by Oleg Volk.

completed a concealed carry class that you are anywhere near prepared to use your defensive firearm to defend yourself. Effectively defending your life requires both firearms skill and mental preparation. If you do not understand what I'm talking about, read my blogs on self-defense, take classes on the defensive use of firearms, and read as much as you can on self-defense. A book called *On Killing* by Lt. Col. David Grossman will help you understand how hard it can be to pull the trigger, even when your life is in danger. You will also need to share your acquired information with your family—your spouse, your children, your loved ones—so they too will be prepared for any action you may take. Any family members interested in owning or using a firearm should take training themselves. Qualified firearms instructors will come to your house and help you create a home safety plan, should anything ever happen in your own home. Your home is a place where you can plan more than other locations for what you would do if an intruder enters. You should strategically and safely place firearms in your home, and all family members should have instructions on what to do during and after a home invasion. Again, a qualified firearms instructor can help you in this respect, and can also help prepare your children.

No matter how many hours of firearms training you have accumulated, taking the opportunity to learn more whenever you can is essential to protecting your life and the lives of others.

53

CHOOSING A SELF-DEFENSE ATTORNEY

If you carry for self-defense, and you do not know who to call if you shoot someone, you are 100% unprepared to carry a firearm. What good is defending your life if you do not understand the laws and do not have someone to represent you? If you are not prepared in this manner, you will almost certainly go to jail.

One of the most common requests I receive in firearms classes is from people wanting to keep my cell phone number in their wallet in case they ever need to use their firearm in self-defense. I have created a special program for my clients that gives them 24-hour access to my defense team, but that also encourages and provides education. When we discuss keeping a lawyer's number handy, someone in class has inevitably heard of insurance companies that purport to provide coverage in the event the insured uses deadly force, and the discussion turns to whether those insurance policies are valid and if the affiliated attorneys are good choices. Such insurance companies have been cropping up like daffodils in springtime over the last few years.

The following are a few important points about them:

Your first step should be education—you need to know when and how you can use your firearm to defend yourself or your family. Self-defense laws differ from state to state. This training should go well beyond the training necessary to obtain a concealed carry permit. You need to engage with your instructor in active negotiation scenarios that will make you decide when and if you pull the trigger. You must understand reaction times to help you determine when your life is in jeopardy. You must also consider if you will actually be able to shoot another person. And, if the situation occurs and you shoot, what do you do next? Calling an attorney is only one part of that picture.

In addition to education, you need a qualified defense team. I and other qualified defense attorneys do not work alone. Defending a deadly force case takes a team. Self-defense cases are extremely complex. Ballistics, crime scene investigation, witness interviews, examination of weapons and other physical artifacts, autopsy results and medical reports, review of law enforcement offense and arrest reports, analysis of the physical abilities and limitations of the client and the attacker, as well as background investigations on everyone involved in the incident are key. Make sure the insurance company and affiliated attorney will provide and work with all these experts. I and my attorneys have law degrees, private investigators, and expert witnesses on our side. We understand that while the attorney is important, it takes a team to protect and defend someone who has used their firearm in self-defense. Some organizations have attorneys listed on their "affiliated attorneys" page who have never tried a case. This is not the person you should choose. You need to seek out an attorney who understands the criminal justice system, is a successful trial attorney, a Second Amendment advocate, and who has the experience through prior homicide trials to defend you. A non-gun owner is probably not your best choice if you have the option. If you can find an attorney with all these prerequisites, and who has a team of professionals ready to step in, that person may be a good choice.

You should aggressively interview your potential attorney whom you may need to trust with your freedom and your life. Here is my short list of questions to ask your potential attorney:

- How many cases have you tried as the lead attorney?
- How many homicide / self-defense cases have you tried?
- What education do you have that qualifies you to defend me if I shoot someone?
- What death investigation training do you have?
- Who is on your team?
- What is your firearms experience?
- What is your position on the Second Amendment?

54

How to Tell the Difference Between Homicide and Lawful Deadly Force

Homicide is the act of unlawfully killing another person. Although the definitions vary slightly across the states, and different states may have different "degrees" of homicide, the basic premise is the same: You killed another human being when you should not have. In some states, killing another person may be "manslaughter" or "negligent homicide," which usually carry less punishment because you did not intend to take the human life. Examples of these "lesser" crimes include car wrecks or negligently pulling the trigger on your firearm when you did not intend to do so.

If you actually intend to pull the trigger and kill another person, you are either engaging in behavior that will land you with a homicide conviction or you are engaging in a lawful act of defending your own life or the lives of other people.

The behavior that constitutes the lawful use of deadly force is somewhat state-specific, but general rules apply no matter where you defend yourself. If you reasonably believe that your life is in danger or that you are in danger of serious injury from another person who at the time that you used deadly force had the ability and intent to immediately kill you or cause you serious injury, then you may lawfully defend your life or yourself from that person by using deadly force. In other words, if you are about to die or experience serious harm, and instead of allowing that to happen, you try to kill or seriously harm the person attacking you to stop them from doing the same to you, your behavior does not constitute the crime of homicide.

When you claim that you shot another person in self-defense, you are stating that you purposefully pulled the trigger in compliance with the law. Your behavior was a lawful reaction to an imminent and deadly threat. If you exclaim in the aftermath of shooting someone that you did not mean to do it, or you cannot believe you did it, or even worse, that you accidentally pulled the trigger, you have created a problem for your defense case. When I am defending someone who claims self-defense, I want to be able to account for every bullet hole in the "bad guy" as a necessary act to stop the threat against my client. If you say something like, "I wanted to teach him a lesson," you are making your case unnecessarily difficult.

When you claim self-defense, you are giving up all other defenses to homicide. You cannot claim negligence and obtain a charge for a lesser offense such as manslaughter. You cannot claim alibi—that it was not you who shot the person. You are claiming that your conduct was intentional and lawful in response to a life-threatening situation. "Excited utterances" that show otherwise can be used against you in court. If you are ever in a situation where you use deadly force, limiting what you say and to whom is extremely important. Do not try to explain yourself to others, especially bystanders or the press, who may arrive on scene.

In addition, you cannot claim self-defense if you are committing a felony, engaged in mutual combat, or started the fight. You must, as we say in legal terminology, have "clean hands." You must be an innocent victim who had no choice but to be killed, maimed, or pull the trigger.

55

THE LIFE OF A CRIMINAL CASE

Criminal cases begin with an investigation. Law enforcement officers will collect as much evidence as they can about a shooting. They will collect items such as your firearm, the expended cartridges, and any other weapons involved, such as your attacker's knife. They will take fingerprints. They will submit samples to the crime lab to collect scientific evidence. They will collect the autopsy report of anyone who died in the incident. They will interview all witnesses and collect reports from other professionals on scene, such as the first responders (EMTs and paramedics). They might ask to interview you (and you need to know how to handle this).

After law enforcement officers have collected all the evidence they believe possible, they will write reports for their supervising officers to approve. Those reports are ultimately submitted to the prosecuting attorney's office. The prosecuting attorney assigned to the case will review the reports and make a decision on what action to take next. The prosecuting attorney usually takes one of three actions at this point: 1) requests that the officers conduct some additional investigation (such as interview additional witnesses or send evidence to a crime lab for additional testing); 2) charges the case by signing an Information or scheduling the case for grand jury; or 3) declining prosecution. The prosecuting attorney can take months or even years to decide whether or not to proceed with a case. Your firearm will be held as potential evidence until the prosecuting attorney makes a decision on your case.

If a case is declined for prosecution, you are likely cleared of ever being charged with a crime. However, there is generally no deadline for a prosecutor to file homicide charges against someone. The charge can be filed at any time.

Prosecutors often have a choice whether to submit a case to a grand jury or file charges and schedule a preliminary hearing. In either instance, the point of the grand jury and the preliminary hearing is to provide a system to ensure that there is enough evidence against someone to proceed with a felony charge.

If a case is submitted to the grand jury, a panel of citizens will be called together to hear evidence and determine whether criminal charges should be filed. Grand jury procedures vary by state. Sometimes, grand juries meet in secret, where prospective defendants are not entitled to be present at the proceedings and no one is allowed to cross-examine witnesses on the defendant's behalf. In secret grand jury proceedings, information presented to the grand jury is presented by prosecuting attorneys. Other times, grand juries may meet to hear from both sides, or their proceedings are recorded.

The grand jury has broad investigative powers and may require that witnesses appear before it and answer the grand jury's questions.

If the grand jury determines that criminal proceedings

should be initiated, it returns (signs) a document called an "indictment."

Based on this indictment, a judge will either issue a summons or an arrest warrant for the person accused of the crime. The person charged with a crime then appears before the court to hear the charges at an arraignment. Effectively, the grand jury process eliminates the necessity for the preliminary hearing, where defendants are always notified and may appear.

After a person is arraigned on a criminal charge (arraigned means the court read them their rights and officially advised them of the charges against them), they will either be held in custody (jail) or released with conditions on what they may do and where they may go while their case is pending. Typically, the accused person's attorney will simultaneously prepare the client's case for trial and attempt to obtain a favorable plea bargain from the prosecuting attorney. This process involves an exchange of information between the prosecutor and the defense attorney known as "discovery." The discovery process is designed to force both sides to show each other their "hand." This process is supposed to prevent unnecessary trials (and unnecessary surprise at trials that could cause further delays in the process) and encourage the parties to the case to settle if possible. Sometimes, the discovery process helps a guilty person accept a plea bargain or causes the prosecuting attorney to dismiss the case.

If the case is negotiated, it is set for a time for the accused to appear before the court and enter a plea. If the case is not negotiated, it is set for trial.

If the jury finds the defendant guilty or if the defendant

pleads guilty, the case is set for a sentencing hearing. The sentencing hearing is where some, limited, evidence may be presented to encourage the court to shorten or lengthen the defendant's sentence. Some states allow juries to decide a sentence in certain circumstances. If a jury finds the defendant not guilty of the charges, then the case is over, the defendant is "acquitted," and there is no conviction on the defendant's record.

After a defendant is sentenced, there may be appeals or other, post-conviction proceedings. The above is a very simplified time-line to give you a sense of how a criminal case proceeds through the criminal justice system.

56

BRANDISHING & WARNING SHOTS: REALLY BAD IDEAS

It should go without saying for gun owners that if you hear something from the White House under the current administration, you ought to be questioning its validity. When Vice President Biden announced after the Sandy Hook school shooting that the best defense for a woman is to fire a few warning shots from a shotgun from her balcony, gun experts and law enforcement shook their heads at the absurdity of that statement. Why? Because brandishing a firearm or firing warning shots means your life is in danger, but you are not taking action to protect it. Even worse, you are putting other lives in danger and committing a crime.

The United States Code defines brandishing as "[D]isplay[ing] all or part of the firearm, or otherwise mak[ing] the presence of the firearm known to another person, in order to intimidate that person, regardless of whether the firearm is directly visible to that person."[133] Most states have a similar state law. Put plainly, brandishing is when one person reveals a firearm to another person to intimidate the other person.

If you are under attack, your life is either in imminent danger or it is not. Brandishing your firearm will often only escalate the situation or get you charged with the crime of brandishing.

Many gun owners ask me when confronted by a threat whether they should let the attacker know they are armed. They assume if they show the other person their gun, the other person will turn and run. Unfortunately, any person threatening your life is generally not mentally stable. Because they are not *acting* like a normal person, you cannot expect them to *react* like a normal person. Rather, if you show them your gun, their abnormal behavior will often only intensify. Showing a person your firearm under these circumstances with the hope you will not have to use it, will likely make a bad situation worse, and cause your attacker to become more enraged. I have personally defended gun owners to whom this has happened—they pulled out their firearms only to have the situation escalate—sometimes to the point of someone getting shot. Law enforcement officers routinely experience this as well.

An attacker is likely to try to take your gun so he can use it against you if you simply brandish it and do not demonstrate positive control. The attacker can very easily succeed in this effort if you are not 100% prepared to either draw your weapon and pull the trigger or otherwise manage the situation. A person can attack you in a fraction of a second, and you are probably not prepared if you are just "showing" them you have a gun. If you are being threatened, you are not going to know whether the sight of your gun will deter the criminal or enrage him. The wrong result could be deadly for you, or even result in your own arrest and criminal prosecution.

Gun owners need training in de-escalating a situation without threatening the person who is threatening you. Very often, retaliating with threats escalates situations to the level of physical confrontation. If you have not been trained to negotiate when the situation allows for it, you need to seek out such training. Brandishing a gun is not the answer.

Similarly, if you fire a warning shot, you will very likely be charged with a crime.

This would be the case whether your life is in imminent danger or not. The same reasoning outlined above with regard to brandishing a firearm applies to warning shots. Whenever you fire a gun, you should ALWAYS have an intended target and know where your bullet is going to go. Never, never fire a gun into the air or in a random direction, because you never know what (or who) it will hit.

If you are justified in drawing your firearm, you should be pointing it at the person who may be killing you in just a few seconds rather than pointing it in the air and trying to scare someone who is mentally unstable. Abnormal people rarely act normally in response to your threats. Instead, they will most often continue to engage you and attempt to carry out their own goals, which may include robbing you, raping you, or killing you.

Police interviews (or cross-examinations by prosecutors at trial) of the shooter after the gun owner has fired the gun will almost always include a question about what the gun owner was thinking when he or she 1) pulled out their firearm, 2) pointed the firearm, and 3) pulled the trigger. If your answer to each one of these questions is not that you believed your life was in danger, you have a problem with your defense. Put another way, if you did not believe your life or the life of the person you were protecting was in danger, or that you were in imminent danger of serious bodily injury, you were not justified in using deadly force.

57

IF YOU OWN A SELF-DEFENSE FIREARM, YOU NEED TO BE MENTALLY PREPARED TO KILL ANOTHER PERSON

Some people, I have learned, are offended by the word "kill." I have people argue with me that they do not ever intend to kill anyone, even though they have purchased a firearm for self-defense purposes.

I sometimes use the word "kill" in my writings because while it might be harsh, it is what very well may happen. I try to instill the harshness of that reality in people to force them to think about that fact. It doesn't matter if you take that human life because the person first tried to kill you. You are still going to experience an extremely traumatic event, compounded with living the rest of your life knowing you are responsible for having taken someone else's life.

I have spent ample time in discussion with people who have pulled the trigger because they felt they had no other choice if they were to save their own life. The resulting emotions that someone feels after shooting another human, even if you do not kill the other person, are profound. If you own a gun for use as a self-defense tool, you may purposefully try to kill another person, and you need to be prepared before and during the situation to do it and to deal with your emotions afterward. This is not an easy task.

It is important to comprehend and face the emotions you will be dealing with before a deadly force situation occurs. You should complete training on this topic as soon as possible and research the problems you may encounter with taking another life.

On Killing by Lt. Col. David Grossman is an excellent read and will help you mentally prepare for such an act. If you realize through your training that you will have trouble pulling the trigger in a life or death situation, you either need more training and preparation, or you should not keep a firearm for self-defense.

58

YOUR HOME IS YOUR CASTLE, BUT THE INTRUDER STILL HAS RIGHTS

Under what circumstances can you kill another person to protect human life? Unfortunately, there is no one answer, as the right to take life in an effort to save life varies according to the jurisdiction where you pull the trigger. The lawful use of deadly force also depends upon all of the facts of the situation that caused you to make that decision.

A "castle doctrine" provides gun owners with special protection inside their homes and sometimes in their vehicles or places of work. Think, "My home is my castle," and you get the point. You may be able to take human life to protect yourself inside your home, but, given the same circumstances in another building, you may be committing murder.

As a preliminary matter, there is a difference between a "castle doctrine" and a "stand your ground" law. Castle doctrine refers to the ability of a homeowner to use deadly force to defend himself, herself or other people inside the home. Some states expand the castle doctrine to other locations, such as a vehicle or place of work, and give special rules about when deadly force can be used in those special locations. In contrast, stand your ground laws refer to the laws that allow you to use deadly force in self-defense in any location in which you are legally allowed to be, rather than turn and run.

The State of Florida has one of the most protective castle doctrines in the country. Why? Because rather than make the shooter prove that he or she acted reasonably in self-defense, Florida's statute presumes that a person acted reasonably when the shooter (victim) uses deadly force against someone (criminal) who is unlawfully and forcefully entering the victim's home or car. In other words, if you shoot an intruder breaking into your house, you are PRESUMED to have acted lawfully in shooting that person. What a concept—let's trust the law abiding citizen to have made the right decision in a split second when discovering that another, unauthorized person is in their house rather than making the homeowner (victim) prove that they acted reasonably when fearing for his or her own life, or the lives of children.

A homeowner who is presumed to be acting in self-defense if the homeowner shoots an uninvited person with no legal right to be in the homeowner's residence has a distinct advantage in a deadly force situation. If you live in Florida and you hear a noise in the middle of the night and find an unknown person in your kitchen—you may be able to lawfully shoot that person in self-defense. In comparison, if the same situation occurs in a state without a protective castle doctrine, the homeowner may have to articulate that the unknown person in the kitchen threatened his or her life. Finding out after the fact that the person you shot was your drunk neighbor who mistakenly wound up bumbling around inside your house will mean prison time for you in many states, because you must be able to articulate that the person you shot intended to seriously harm you. The fact that the person you shot was inside your house uninvited is usually not enough to justify the use of deadly force against that person.

Gun owners need to be aware that not all states have castle doctrines and that the protection afforded by castle doctrines are state specific. You need to learn every state's castle doctrine where you may "reside" or be "domiciled" and in any other state in which you possess a firearm with the intent to use it for self-defense. Words like "reside" and "domiciled" should be defined under the applicable state's laws. For example, some states may define "reside" as a place where you stay the night, while others may define the word more specifically to describe the place where you live. It is important to know these laws before you carry a self-defense firearm in the applicable location.

59

TURN & RUN OR STAND YOUR GROUND?

Different from a castle doctrine, a stand your ground law (also known as a duty to retreat law) applies anywhere you may find your life is threatened—inside your home or not. These laws specify whether you must turn and run if it is safe to do so, or if you may stand your ground and defend yourself (or another person) whenever and wherever your life may be threatened.

If you are threatened in a grocery store parking lot while standing by your car with the driver's side door open, and you

Photo by Oleg Volk.

realize you could get in the car and drive away, a stand your ground law may protect you if you instead decide to pull your handgun from its holster, stand your ground, and defend your life using deadly force. Determining whether to stand your ground or retreat can be an extremely difficult decision to make in a split-second. Stand your ground laws are designed to protect gun owners who err on the side of caution and use deadly force.

Like all self-defense laws, stand your ground laws also differ between states. Responsible gun owners must research stand your ground laws wherever they may live or travel with a firearm.

60

WHY YOU SHOULD USE THE SAME AMMUNITION AS LAW ENFORCEMENT

The ammunition you use to stop a threat may be criticized by ignorant people because it is deadly. However, this is exactly what you want and need to use to be effective and not hurt innocent people. Law enforcement officers use hollow-point bullets because they are deadly and because these bullets are less likely than ordinary bullets to penetrate walls or other objects and kill or injure an innocent person. For your self-defense case, it will help if your attorney can tell the jury that when you decided to own a deadly weapon, you researched what ammunition your local law enforcement agency uses to best protect the public,

Hollow point bullets. Photo by Oleg Volk.

and chose the same brand and type so you were acting as safely and responsibly as possible. Of course, for some gun owners, the law of their jurisdiction has limited their ability to use protective ammunition, such as hollow point bullets. Make sure your ammunition is legal in the location where you may use it.

Hollow point bullets. Photo by Oleg Volk.

61

IF YOU USE YOUR FIREARM IN SELF-DEFENSE, YOU ARE THE VICTIM

When I teach self-defense classes, I always ask my students, "You have just shot someone who is laying in a pool of blood and dying right in front of you. Who is the victim?" Most people say the poor guy who is dying. Wrong answer.

Do not let the pool of blood your would-be killer is dying in fool you. Keep your mind focused on the fact that your life was just endangered, which forced you to take action and behave in a way you would have preferred to avoid. You had to take that person's life. If you did not, he would have taken yours. He is not and was not the victim. He was the instigator. Because you are the victim, you should act like the victim. You will not turn and run. You will not act like a hardened criminal and refuse any conversation with the cops. Instead, you will make a brief statement to law enforcement. Most importantly, you will call 9-1-1 and report that a crime has been committed against YOU.

In my gun-related classes, I teach my students what to report and when to stop talking. I provide example 9-1-1 calls. It is impossible to anticipate the exact situation a gun owner may be in, but the more you plan and prepare, the more likely it is you will do the right things in the aftermath of a shooting. There is nothing wrong with having an idea of what you will tell 9-1-1 and the first officers on the scene. In fact, it is essential that you have a good idea as to what you will say and do, so you will instinctively say and do those things if the situation arises. Knowing that you will tell 9-1-1 operators and officers who arrive on scene that 1) you were attacked; 2) your life was in danger, and 3) you are too emotional to give a detailed interview but will cooperate as soon as you speak with your attorney, are key.

62

You Are the Primary Scene Manager

Imagine the chaos after a person has been shot. People are afraid and they scatter. Some of them will be witnesses who can corroborate your story. Instead of staying, they run and choose not to get involved. Paramedics arrive on the scene focusing on the person in need of medical attention (hopefully, your attacker, not you). Despite good intentions and best efforts, evidence such as shell casings from the shots your attacker fired at you or the attacker's knife or other items that corroborate your story, may be kicked and lost in the turmoil.

You cannot rely on first responders and law enforcement to know your story. You have to rely on YOU. You will see and experience things that others did not. You cannot allow anyone to move any evidence. You must be strong until you have pointed out the witnesses and the evidence to the responding officers.

Try to remember that you are responsible for preserving the scene and pointing out locations of events and evidence to the officers.

63

UNDERSTANDING THE POLICE POWER TO SEARCH, SEIZE, AND ARREST

Laws for and against gun owners are being enacted all over the country. Rights and responsibilities are under extreme scrutiny. Some people call 9-1-1 if they see a person with a gun. Some private businesses or governmental agencies promote this practice.

If you are lawfully carrying a gun, on campus or elsewhere, you are not committing a crime and should not be subject to answering to law enforcement. However, some states require that you disclose that you have a firearm if you are contacted by a law enforcement officer. In addition, there is a rule of law that allows a law enforcement officer to stop a person to determine whether they are committing a crime if the officer has "reasonable articulable suspicion" that the person is committing, is about to commit, or has committed a crime. While the act of lawfully carrying a gun should no more constitute reasonable articulable suspicion of criminal activity than lawfully driving a car, it appears that some officials will interpret the law in that manner.

If you are stopped by a law enforcement officer, you have rights—and a law enforcement officer must be able to tell a judge what specific facts gave him the suspicion that you were engaged in criminal activity.

If you are stopped, you should ask if you are free to leave. If the officer says yes, you should calmly and silently walk away. If the officer says no, you have a right to know why, because you are either being detained or arrested. You have the right to remain silent and cannot be punished for refusing to answer questions. Many people tend to want to be helpful, and they think that giving consent to an officer to search them or engaging in dialogue with an officer will help them improve the situation. This well-intentioned behavior is not required.

While you do not have to consent to a search of yourself or any belongings, officers may "pat down" your clothing if they have reasonable articulable suspicion to stop you for criminal activity, suspect a weapon, and suspect that you are presently dangerous. You should not physically resist, but you do have the right to refuse consent for any further search. Keep in mind that the reasonable articulable suspicion required to pat you down must be that you are armed and dangerous. In other words, that the officer has legitimate reason for believing you may use that weapon *unlawfully*. Remaining calm and being polite will help you counter that suspicion, as opposed to acting in an angry and threatening manner.

If you are asked to provide your identification, you must do so if you are driving a car in most states. However, if you are not driving a car, the law in some states is unsettled on whether or not you must provide your identification. In most circumstances, it makes sense to do so, even if you are correct and the officer is wrong. The reasons are that you do not want to escalate the situation and find yourself arrested for disturbing the peace or some other crime, and if the officer has no right to ask for your ID to begin with, you will walk away after the encounter and contact an attorney for advice on how to proceed.

If you are stopped and patted down for carrying a gun, you may have a legal claim against the law enforcement agency for violating your civil liberties. You should maintain your composure throughout the encounter, and contact an attorney to report the violation.

The Fourth Amendment protects our right to privacy by preventing unreasonable searches and seizures. Government agents must generally have "probable cause" to search you, your home, your car, a bag or any other item that belongs to you or is in your possession, such as a laptop or cell phone. If an officer has probable cause that he or she will find evidence of criminal activity, the officer must generally obtain a search warrant, which is signed by a judge authorizing the search, or they must justify an exception to the warrant requirement. As a District Attorney, I frequently helped write, review, and approve search warrants. The bottom line is that officers must provide solid, reliable evidence detailing what they believe they will find, where they expect to find it, and why they expect to find it, before they can lawfully conduct a search. There are, however, exceptions to the search warrant requirement.

The most common exceptions include consent (the officer asks if he or she can look in your bag and you give them permission), the person is arrested and the officer conducts a search incident to arrest (a search for items on the arrested person that could be dangerous), or the officer can justify a search due to exigent (emergency) circumstances. The most important thing to remember as a gun owner is that unless the officer has a warrant or can articulate an exception to the warrant requirement, he or she cannot legally search you or your belongings, nor are you required to consent to a search.

64
Your Doctor's Right to Search, or Not

After Congress passed the Affordable Care Act in 2010, doctors became emboldened about asking patients for information regarding their personal firearms. Surprising to most gun owners, the Affordable Care Act actually included language meant to protect Second Amendment rights. This is because our current laws prohibit the government from collecting data about gun owners unless government officials are investigating criminal activity and they navigate through the proper channels (such as getting a search warrant) to obtain the information they seek.

The Affordable Care Act did not change this protection, and while the current administration would like it to be different, the government cannot require that information regarding gun ownership be disclosed to physicians, and gun ownership cannot be used to determine insurance premium rates. However, some private doctors have made the decision to begin creating records on their own initiative.

The same law that instituted federal regulation of retail firearms sales in the United States, and which law requires dealers to keep records of all firearms made, imported, acquired or disposed of, also protects individual gun owners. This law is the Gun Control Act of 1968, and one of the central Congressional compromises in passing the Act was that the collected gun ownership records would be kept by the dealers, not by the federal, state, or local governments. A subsequent federal law, the Firearms Owners' Protection Act of 1986, expanded the protection to individual gun owners by preventing any governmental body from passing a rule or regulation that would require centralization of federally mandated dealer records, or require establishment of any system of registration of firearms, firearms owners, or firearms transactions or disposition.

If your doctor asks you about guns in your home, do you have to answer? If you believe the question is pertinent to your treatment, you may choose to answer it. A doctor cannot compel you to answer the question, and if a doctor chooses to turn you away for your refusal to answer the question, choose another doctor. You may even be able to sue the doctor who refused to provide you treatment.

In fact, after repeated cases of doctors refusing to treat patients who denied doctors their personal gun ownership information, the State of Florida took action against anti-gun doctors by passing the Firearms Owner's Privacy Act.[134] This Act prevents doctors from asking patients about firearm ownership and prevents them from keeping a record of their patients' guns unless the physician can show that the information is necessary for a patient's medical treatment.

Shortly after the law went into effect, a group of doctors filed suit against the State of Florida, claiming that the law violates the First and Fourteenth Amendments of the United States Constitution; however, the 11th Circuit Court of Appeals disagreed, and upheld the Act as constitutional. In its 77 page written opinion, the Court wrote that the Act "codifies the commonsense conclusion that good medical care does not require inquiry or record-keeping regarding firearms when unnecessary to a patient's care—especially not when that inquiry or record-keeping constitutes such a substantial intrusion upon patient privacy."[135]

So for now, absent the abuse of power by our intelligence agencies, our laws are designed to protect gun owners and prevent a government created database of firearm owners. Of course, there are lawmakers who would prefer to change these laws. It is your duty as a citizen to be informed, watch the proposals, and actively participate to prevent any such laws from being passed in the future. For now, guard your personal information and be aware that you are not required to disclose that personal information just because someone asks you a question.

65

SUMMARY

The preceding chapters are basic things every gun owner should know. Responsible gun owners still should know more. I and my partners teach specialized courses on different aspects of gun ownership, including possession and transfer laws, awareness, the use of deadly force, and scene management after a shooting.

This book was written to provide you with tips you should consider and use to seek out additional training. It is YOUR responsibility as a gun owner to know basic self-defense, possession, and transfer laws before you own a firearm for self-defense purposes.

My advice is simple. Seek out training as well as an attorney who is well-versed in criminal and civil gun laws and who supports the Second Amendment. Not all attorneys and instructors are equal. I have witnessed a judge throw an attorney off of a murder case because the attorney was doing such a poor job for his client. As a gun owner, you need to screen and secure your self-defense attorney before an incident ever happens.

I sincerely hope the information in this book is helpful to you. I encourage you to share it with your fellow gun owners in the hopes that more responsible gun owners, like yourself, will care enough to read it and act responsibly, as you have. I will write periodically about each of these items on my Gun Law bLAWg and address various topics in the Gun Law Podcast as well, so I hope you stop by and leave a comment or two about your own situation or one you have heard about. The more we can share stories with each other, the more we will learn.

I am very active in social media, as you can see from my website, *www.alexkincaidlaw.com*. If you are on Facebook, Twitter, LinkedIn, or Instagram, please reach out and connect with me or follow me so you can stay in touch with all the other topics I will write about in the near future.

If there are other topics you would be interested in learning about, please let me know either through an e-mail or a comment on our "Contact Us" page on the Alex Kincaid Law website at *www.alexkincaidlaw.com*. We love to hear your thoughts, ideas, and suggestions. Please let me know how I can help you and your loved ones be safer and protect your lives! Thank you.

The author, holding MCM Firearms' "Idaho Liberty Belle" rifle at the Idaho State Capitol. Photo by Josh Wolfe.

[1]   Some excellent choices on the history and meaning of the Second Amendment include Stephen P. Halbrook, That Every Man Be Armed (2013); Clayton E. Cramer, Armed America (2006); Clayton E. Cramer, For the Defense of Themselves and the State, The original Intent and Judicial Interpretation of the Right to Keep and Bear Arms (1994).

[2]   U.S. Const. art. II, § 1, cl. 1.

[3]   U.S. Const. art. II, § 3.

[4]   U.S. Const. art. II, § 2, cl. 1.

[5]   Exec. Order No. 9,066, 7 Fed. Reg. 1, 407.

[6]   Exec. Order No. 13,223, 66 Fed. Reg. 48201.

[7]   Exec. Order No 13,224, 66 Fed Reg. 49079.

[8]   Exec. Order No. 12,228, 66 Fed.Reg. 51812.

[9]   Although history shows this rarely happens. See Anderson, Leanna M. 2002. "Executive Orders, 'The Very Definition of Tyranny,' and the Congressional Solution, and the Separation of Powers Restoration Act." *Hastings Constitutional Law Quarterly* 29 (spring): 589-611.

[10]   U.S. Const. art. VI, cl. 2.

[11]   See Fl. St. § 790.33.

[12]   In an episode of the Gun Law Podcast, I spoke with Miko Tempski, General Counsel for the Second Amendment Foundation and Greg Pruett, President and Founder of the Idaho Second Amendment Alliance about their preemption projects – the successes, the failures, and the potential lawsuits. My guests provided insight on the process and information on how to contact their organizations to report a violation of a state preemption law and how to support their efforts. All episodes of the Gun Law Podcast, including this one, are available on my website at www.AlexKincaidLaw.com.

[13]   Believe it or not, "destructive device" even has its own definition, so it doesn't include things like hammers, wrecking balls, or toddlers. And by now, you shouldn't be surprised to know that the definition is different under the GCA than it is under the NFA.

[14]   I.C. § 19-2520.

[15]   Justice Louis Brandeis coined this term in *New State Ice Co. v. Liebmann*, 285 U.S. 262 (1932), long after our Founding Fathers were gone, but he accurately captured the essence of their intentions with this phrase.

[16]   U.S. Const. amend. II.

[17]   *Dist. of Columbia v. Heller*, 554 U.S. 570, 626 (2008).

[18]   *Mance v. Holder*, No. 14-539-O, 2015 U.S. Dist. Lexis 16679 (N.D. Tex. Feb. 11, 2015).

[19]   18 U.S.C. § 922(g)(8).

[20]   *Heller, supra* note 17.

[21]   The petitioner is the party that initiates an action before a court. The respondent is the party against whom the action is being brought. In this case, the petitioner was Washington D.C.

[22]   *Heller,* 554 U.S. at 630.

[23]   The most definitive source to help understand the Founding Fathers' intent for many aspects of the Constitution, including the Second Amendment, is a series of 85 essays called *The Federalist Papers,* which were written by three of our Founding Fathers between 1787 and 1788, to encourage the citizens of New York to ratify (approve) the Constitution. New York's ratification was critical to getting the Constitution accepted and put in place to serve as the supreme governing document for the United States of America.

[24]   The prefatory clause is the first part of the Second Amendment: "A well regulated militia being necessary to the security of a free State"

[25]   *Heller,* 554 U.S. at 627.

[26]   *Id.* at 636.

[27]   *McDonald v. Chicago,* 561 U.S. 742 (2010).

[28]   *Peruta v. Cnty. of San Diego,* 742 F.3d 1144, 1166-1167 (9th Cir. 2014).

[29]   Kruschke, Earl R., Gun Control: A Reference Handbook (1995).

[30]   Interview with Jillair Kubish, former Director of Industry Operations, the ATF (April 22, 2015).

[31]   *John Lott, interview with Timothy H. Lee, July 22, 2010, available at http://cfif.org/v/index.php/commentary/42-constitution-and-legal/686-john-lott-more-guns-still-less-crime.*

[32]   Elliott Rodger.

[33] $3551.42; Bureau of Labor Statistics, CPI Inflation Calculator, www.bls.gov/data/inflation-calculator.htm.

[34]   U.S. Dept. of Justice, Bureau of Alcohol, Tobacco, Firearms and Explosives, A.T.F. National Firearms Act Handbook: Section No. 2.1.6. (A.T.F. E-Publication 5320.8). Office of Enforcement Programs & Services, Rev. April 2009; 18 U.S.C. 921(r); 26 U.S.C. § 5845.

[35]   U.S. Dept. of Justice, Bureau of Alcohol, Tobacco, Firearms and Explosives, A.T.F. National Firearms Act Handbook: Section No. 2.1.8.2 (A.T.F. E-Publication 5320.8). Office of Enforcement Programs & Services, Rev. April 2009.

[36]   ATF Rul. 2001-1, February 2, 2001.

[37]   ATF Commerce in Firearms and Ammunition, 27 CRF 478.11 (2012).

38 *U.S. v. Cash*, 149 F.3d 706 (C.A.7 (Ill.) 1998).

39 ATF Rul. 81-4.

40 26 U.S.C. § 5845(b).

41 *Cash*, 149 F.3d at 707-708.

42 18 U.S.C. §§ 921-931 (2006).

43 Gun Control Act of 1968, Public Law 90-618, Title 18, U.S.C. Firearms, Ch.44 § 101 (1968).

44 U.S. Const. art. 1, § 8, cl. 3.

45 18 U.S.C. § 921(a)(21)(A)&(B).

46 18 U.S.C. § 921(a)(21)(C).

47 18 U.S.C. § 921(a)(21)(D).

48 18 U.S.C. § 921(a)(12).

49 18 U.S.C. § 921(a)(21)(E)&(F).

50 18 U.S.C. § 921(a)(21)(C).

51 18 U.S.C. § 921(a)(21)(D).

52 27 C.F.R. 478.39.

53 http://www.atf.gov/publications/factsheets/factsheet-national-tracing-center.html

54 *Soto et al v. Bushmaster Firearm Int'l, LLC., et al*, No. 3:2015cv00068 (D.Conn., 2015).

55 *U.S. v. McLemore*, 792 F. Supp. 96, 98 (S.D. Ala. 1992).

56 *Obergefell v. Hodges*, No. 14-556, (U.S. June 26, 2014)(Justia).

57 Open Letter to All Federal Firearms Licensees, U.S. Dept. of Justice – Bureau of Alcohol, Tobacco, Firearms and Explosives, (September 21, 2011). http://vcic.vermont.gov/sites/vcic/files/US%20DOJ%20Open%20Letter%20to%20All%20Federal%20Firearms%20Licensees%202011.pdf (last visited August 31, 2015)

58 *U.S. v. Purdy*, 264 F.2d 809, 812-13 (9th Cir. 2001) (court upheld conviction because defendant used drugs two days before firearm seized because of witness testimony indicating his continued drug use).

59 27 C.F.R. § 478.11.

60 Again, proper trust planning can prevent this situation.

61 After getting involved locally, it became apparent to me that the gun laws are as much as mystery to the workers in these fields as in any other.

62 27 C.F.R. § 478.11.

63 See my Gun Law Podcast with Clayton E. Cramer for more on the mental illness issues.

64 Robert J. Epley, Director, Compensation and Pension Service, to All VBA Regional Offices and Centers, June 2, 2000, Subj.: National Instant Criminal Background Check System (NICS) Process.

65 at https://forms.fbi.gov/nics-appeal-request-form.

66 18 U.S.C. § 921(20)(a).

67 18 U.S.C. § 922(g)(1); regulations regarding executive clemency by pardon are found at 28 C.F.R. § 1.1, 1.2.

68 *U.S. v. Smith*, 940 F.2d 395, 396 (C.A. 9 (Cal.) 1990).

69 27 C.F.R. §478.144.

70 18 U.S.C. § 925(c).

71 28 C.F.R. § 0.130(a)(1).

72 *See* Treasury, Postal Service, and General Government Appropriations Act, 1993, Pub. L. No. 102-393, 106 Stat. 1729, 1732; Consolidated Appropriations Act, 2014, Pub. L. No. 113-No. 13-1876.

73 In 2008, Congress passed An Act to Improve the National Instant Criminal Background Check system, P.L. 100-180, 122 Stat. 2559 (2008).

74 *Tyler v. Hillsdale County Sheriff's Dept., et. al.*, 775 F.3d 308 (2014).

75 *Id.* at 334.

76 "Right to Keep and Bear Arms: Report of the Subcommittee on the Constitution of the Committee on the Judiciary, United States Senate, Ninety-seventh Congress, Second Session" (PDF). *constitution.org*. Constitution Society. Retrieved July 5, 2014. A more accessible facsimile of the 1982 Senate subcommittee report.

77 18 U.S.C. ch. 44 § 921 et seq.

78 Kruschke, Earl R. *Gun Control: A Reference Handbook* (1995).

79 IACP/LEIM eTRACE-FTS". BATFE (The IACP). 2010-06-03. p. 38.

80 ATF Fact Sheet, May 2014, available at https://www.atf.gov/file/11181/download (last visited 9/6/2015).

81 *Ambramski v. U.S.*, No. 12-1493 (U.S. June 16, 2014)(Justia).

82 If not, you can learn more about it at http://www.dontlie.org.

83 *Ambramski, supra* note 74.

84 In violation of § 922(a)(6).

85 In violation of § 924(a)(1)(A).

86 You can keep up to date on the changing laws by subscribing to the Gun Law Podcast and by visiting www.AlexKincaidLaw.com.

87 John R. Lott, Jr., More Guns Less Crime, 327 (University of Chicago Press, 3rd ed. 2010).

88 18. U.S.C. 921(a)(30).

89 CA. Att'y Gen., Assault Weapons Identification Guide: as listed or described in Penal Code Sections 12276, 12276.1, and 12276.5 (3rd ed. 2001).

90 18 U.S.C. 921(a)(30).

91 C.R.S. § 18-12-301; C.R.S. § 18-12-302; and C.R.S. § 18-12-112.

92 2013 Conn. Pub. Act 13-3, as amended by 2013 Conn. Pub. Act 13-220; Conn. Gen. Stat. §§ 53-202a–53-202f.

93 *N.Y. State Rifle and Pistol Ass'n, Inc.*, No. 14-36-cv (2nd Cir., October 9, 2015).

94 Act of January 15, 2013, ch. 1, 2013 N.Y. Laws, amended by Act of Mar. 29, 2013, ch. 57, pt. FF 2013 N.Y. Laws 290, 389.

95 *N.Y. State Rifle and Pistol Ass'n.*, Inc. at 43-44.

96 Available at http://www.nraila.org/gun-laws/state-laws.aspx.

97 https://www.atf.gov/publications/firearms/state-laws/31st-edition/index.html (visited October 10, 2015).

98 18 U.S.C. § 922(x)(2).

99 *National Rifle Association, et al v. Bureau of Alcohol, Tobacco, et al*, No. 11-10959 (5th Cir. 2012, Revised 2013), available at http://www.ca5.uscourts.gov/opinions/pub/11/11-10959-CV0.wpd.pdf.

100 18 U.S.C. § 922 (2), (5).

101 18 U.S.C. § 922(x)(3)(emphasis added).

102 20 U.S.C. § 7151.

103 Fl. Stat. § 1006.07(g).

104 H.R. 2625 (113th): Student Protection Act.

105 See, e.g., I.C. § 18-3302B.

106 Cal. Pen. Code § 25105.

107 18 U.S.C. § 930.

108 18 U.S.C. § 930(d).

109 16 U.S.C. § 1a-7b; 50 C.F.R. § 27.41.

110 36 C.F.R. § 261.10(d).

111 43 C.F.R. § 8365.2-5.

112 18 U.S.C. §922(q)(1)(A).

113 The GFSZA includes exceptions for:

1) firearms on private property (including homes used for home schooling as the law is currently interpreted);

2) unloaded firearms in a locked container or locked firearms rack in a motor vehicle;

3) unloaded firearms possessed while traversing school grounds to access hunting land;

4) entry authorized by the school;

5) persons licensed by state or local authorities;

6) individuals using a firearm in a school program;

7) law enforcement officers acting in an official capacity.

Note that under these exceptions, an individual who has been issued a right-to-carry license by the state, or a political subdivision of the state, in which the "school zone" is located, may continue to carry in a "school zone" in compliance with existing state and local laws. Non-licensed individuals who drive through a "school zone" must have their firearms unloaded and locked in a container or firearms rack.

[114] There is currently no mechanism to restore the gun rights for an individual who has been convicted of a federal offense.

[115] *U.S. v. Lopez*, 514 U.S. 549 (1995).

[116] 18 U.S.C. §922(q)(2)(A).

[117] John R. Lott, CPRC at Fox News Gun Free Zones an Easy Target for Killers, Crime Prevention Research Center (June 18, 2015). Available at http://crimepreventionresearchcenter.org/2015/06/cprc-at-fox-news-gun-free-zones-an-easy-target-for-killers/.

[118] Lott, John R. and Landes, William M., Multiple Victim Public Shootings (October 19, 2000). Available at SSRN: *http://ssrn.com/abstract=272929* or *http://dx.doi.org/10.2139/ssrn.272929*.

[119] Larry Pratt, CEO of the Gun Owners of America, recently sent a plea to gun owners to support Congress's latest attempt to stop the madness by eliminating the GFSZA. GOA remains very active in seeking the repeal of these laws.

[120] According to the United States Department of Labor at https://www.osha.gov/SLTC/workplaceviolence/ 2015.

[121] Available online at https://www.osha.gov/SLTC/workplaceviolence/.

[122] 49 U.S.C. § 46505(b)(1).

[123] 49 C.F.R. § § 1544.201(d); 1544.1(a)(1); 14 C.F.R. § 119.1(a); 14 C.F.R. § 135.119.

[124] 49 C.F.R. § § 1544.201(d); 1544.1(a)(1); 14 C.F.R. § 119.1(a); 14 C.F.R. § 135.119.

[125] 18 U.S.C. §922(e).

[126] See AMTRAK, CHECKED FIREARMS PROGRAM (2010), available at http://www.amtrak.com/firearms-in-checked-baggage and TSA, PROHIBITED ITEMS FOR CHECKED BAGGAGE, available at htt;://www.greyhound.com (last visited October 5, 2015).

127 United Nations Convention on the Law of the Sea: Section No. 4-Contiguous Zone, art. 33 (United Nations) November 16, 1994. Found at http://www.un.org/depts/los/convention_agreements/texts/unclos/part2.htm (last visited 8/30/2015).

128 *People v. Hale*, 43 Cal.App.3d 353, 356 (1974).

129 UPS and FedEx both require that handguns be shipped by "next day air" service.

130 18 U.S.C. § 922(a)(5)(A).

131 Black's Law Dictionary 712 ((the d. 2009).

132 The NFATCA official position on Rule 41P can be read at http://www.nfatca.org/pubs/NFATCA_41P_submission.pdf (last visited 9/13/2015).

133 18 U.S.C. § 924(c)(4).

134 2011 Fla. Laws 112 (codified at Fla. Stat. §§ 381.026, 456.072, 790.338).

135 *Wollschlaeger, et al v. State of Florida, et al*, D.C. Docket No. 1:11-cv-22026-MGC (11th Cir. 2015) at 5.